FIRST TIME IN THE HIGH SCHOOL CLASSROOM

Essential Guide for the New Teacher

Mary C. Clement

ScarecrowEducation
Lanham, Maryland • Toronto • Oxford
2005

Published in the United States of America
by ScarecrowEducation
An imprint of The Rowman & Littlefield Publishing Group, Inc.
4501 Forbes Boulevard, Suite 200, Lanham, Maryland 20706
www.scarecroweducation.com

PO Box 317
Oxford
OX2 9RU, UK

British Library Cataloguing in Publication Information Available

Library of Congress Cataloging-in-Publication Data
Clement, Mary C.
  First time in the high school classroom : essential guide for the
new teacher / Mary C. Clement.
    p. cm.
  Includes bibliographical references and index.
  ISBN 1-57886-197-7 (pbk. : alk. paper)
  1. High school teaching—United States—Handbooks, manuals, etc. 2.
First year teachers—United States—Handbooks, manuals, etc. I. Title.

  LB1737.U6C54 2005
  373.11—dc22

                                                    2004019379

⊗™ The paper used in this publication meets the minimum requirements of
American National Standard for Information Sciences—Permanence of Paper
for Printed Library Materials, ANSI/NISO Z39.48-1992.
Manufactured in the United States of America.

To the teachers at Jacksonville High School,
Jacksonville, Illinois, 1972–1975.
Thank you for my education.

CONTENTS

INTRODUCTION

Imagine walking into an empty classroom with thirty desks and chairs, a chalkboard or whiteboard, and some empty bookcases. Now imagine knowing that every day for the next 180 school days, 143 students will be in your room and you are responsible for ensuring that each one of them learns enough of the subject matter to pass a standardized test given to them in March. In this era of teacher accountability, your continued employment and potential raises may depend on how well your students perform on this test. You will also be expected to help build a homecoming float, chaperone two dances, and coach or supervise at least one extracurricular sport or event this year. Many of your students will come to you for personal advice, perhaps asking where they should attend college, or maybe asking your advice on moving out of their parents' home, getting a job, breaking up with their boyfriend, or having a baby. This is one view of high school teaching, and the question in your mind may be, "Where do I start?"

Before you are given the keys to the empty classroom, some other questions need answering. Why have you become a teacher? Have you prepared in every way you can to be ready for this assignment by completing a teacher certification program and student teaching? Have you gone into teaching because of the teacher shortage and hope to complete teacher certification by taking classes as you teach? What do you say or do when you realize some students may never turn in a homework assignment because they work 40 hours a week at a paying job? What do you say when a student says, "You are the best and I couldn't have graduated without you?"

With or without teacher certification, if you are a new high school teacher, this book is for you. Designed to start at the very beginning, this book covers the essentials of curriculum planning, teaching methods, and managing a high school classroom. It is not a theoretical book, but rather a handbook with essential information to guide you to create your own plans and strategies for teaching. If you completed coursework in curriculum and methods in your teacher preparation program, then this book should review, clarify, and guide you as you start teaching. If you are teaching on a provisional certificate or substitute teaching while working on teacher certification, this book will give you enough basic information not only to survive but to be organized and thrive. The worksheets are models to help you get started; soon you will develop forms for the paperwork and organizational techniques that work best for you. There are examples for different subjects, but again, you must supply the specifics for your field.

Teaching is a very personal endeavor and you may sometimes rely upon what your high school teachers and college instructors did as you make decisions about what to do in your classroom. Before you do so, take a moment and reflect upon the impact of how your teachers taught and how today's students and today's schools may have changed.

Teaching can also be a very lonely endeavor, leaving you feeling isolated if you just shut the door to your room and let yourself be surrounded by students all day. One reminder for a successful year is to create a network of teachers for a support group. After all, you will not be the only math teacher to deal with the quadratic formula this year, or the only English teacher to introduce Longfellow to sophomores. Reach out to other teachers in your building and in your profession for guidance and support. Celebrate your successes at the end of each and every day—and plan another celebration for the end of each semester. Pat yourself on the back when a class goes well, because the day that everything goes perfectly and students actually see the significance of the industrial revolution on the modern age will probably not be the day that the principal completes an evaluation of your history class. Don't forget to congratulate teachers down the hall on their successes as well; maybe you can be an agent of change to lift the morale of the whole school.

While many negatives are mentioned in this introduction, there are tremendous positive reasons for becoming a teacher. Knowing that a student can conduct a scientific experiment and discern when the media misrepresents data, and knowing you taught the student those skills, is indeed fulfilling. Imagine the reward of knowing that you helped a student stay in school and earn a high school diploma. There is no better way to touch the future than to teach young people and help them get started in the world.

So, let's start at the very beginning. You are challenged to teach something to your students and curriculum is the "something" you teach. Good, effective teaching is planned and purposeful, so planning for what to teach is a good place to start.

THE INTERSTATE NEW TEACHER ASSESSMENT AND SUPPORT CONSORTIUM (INTASC) STANDARDS

Whether you just graduated with full licensure or are pursuing alternative certification, your state will have standards for your teaching. The following 10 standards cover what teachers throughout the country are expected to know and to be able to do. Next to each standard you will see a reference to the chapter in this book that covers the material applicable for the standard.

Standard 1: The teacher understands the central concepts, tools of inquiry, and structures of the subject being taught and can create learning experiences that make these aspects of the subject matter meaningful for students.
Chapter 1: Curriculum Planning
Chapter 2: Planning of Lessons, Units, and Syllabi
Standard 2: The teacher understands how children learn and develop, and can provide learning opportunities that support their intellectual, social, and personal development.
Chapter 3: Methods for Teacher Presentations

Standard 3: The teacher understands how students differ in their approaches to learning and creates instructional opportunities that are adapted to diverse learners.
Chapter 3: Methods for Teacher Presentations
Chapter 9: Diversity, Communication with Parents and Community, and Professionalism

Standard 4: The teacher uses various instructional strategies to encourage students' development of critical thinking, problem solving, and performance skills.
Chapter 3: Methods for Teacher Presentations
Chapter 4: Methods for Guiding Student Talk and Thought
Chapter 5: Methods for Guiding Student Production of Work
Chapter 6: Technology and Teaching

Standard 5: The teacher uses an understanding of individual and group motivation and behavior to create a learning environment that encourages positive social interaction, active engagement in learning, and self-motivation.
Chapter 8: Classroom Management and Getting the School Year Started

Standard 6: The teacher uses knowledge of effective verbal, nonverbal, and media communication techniques to foster active inquiry, collaboration, and supportive interaction in the classroom.
Chapter 6: Technology and Teaching
Chapter 8: Classroom Management and Getting the School Year Started

Standard 7: The teacher plans instruction based on knowledge of subject matter, students, the community, and curriculum goals.
Chapter 1: Curriculum Planning
Chapter 2: Planning of Lessons, Units, and Syllabi

Standard 8: The teacher understands and uses formal and informal assessment strategies to evaluate and ensure the continuous intellectual, social, and physical development of the learner.
Chapter 7: Homework, Assessment, and Grading

Standard 9: The teacher is a reflective practitioner who continually evaluates the effects of his or her choices and actions on others (students, parents, and other professionals in the learning community) and who actively seeks out opportunities to grow professionally.

Standard 10: The teacher fosters relationships with school colleagues, parents, and agencies in the larger community to support students' learning and well-being.

①

CURRICULUM PLANNING

Curriculum is what we teach and is the knowledge that the students need to know about the subject. Having earned a degree in your subject matter specialty, you know that there is a knowledge base for your field. Obviously, math teachers know algebra, geometry, trigonometry, and calculus. English teachers know writing and literature. Science teachers know their fields of life or physical science. Knowing your subject prepares you to teach, but who decides what you will actually teach and when you teach each topic? Decades ago, new teachers were simply hired and handed books. The material in those books was the curriculum. Times have changed and the curriculum taught in high schools today is determined by national, state, and local factors.

NATIONAL STANDARDS

Since the late 1980s, national professional organizations for each subject area have established standards in their fields. Simply put, standards are definitions of what students should know and be able to do after taking a course or courses in that subject (Callahan, Clark, & Kellough, 2002). For example, in English, the National Council of Teachers of English, together with the International Reading Association, developed standards for the teaching of English in high schools. You can find out about those standards on the council's website, www.ncte.org. Website information for other organizations include:

- Mathematics: The National Council of Teachers of Mathematics, www.nctm.org
- Science: The National Science Teachers Association, www.nsta.org
- Social studies is divided by fields. Look for specifics for each area, such as standards for economics from the National Council on Economic Education, www.ncee.org, or see information from the National Center for Social Studies, www.socialstudies.org, or the National Center for History in the Schools at www.sscnet.ucla.edu/ nchs for their standards.
- World languages: www.actfl.org

Have the national standards forced all high schools in the United States to teach the same topics in certain grades? Not at all. The national standards are not laws or mandates—and they do not come from the federal government. They are recommendations and guidelines. Book publishers use these guidelines in producing new textbooks in the fields, and state boards of education use them in writing curriculum. For some areas, the standards are quite broad and can be considered vision statements for the teaching of the subject.

STATE STANDARDS

The depth and breadth of each individual state's curriculum standards vary widely. Just as the curriculum documents vary by state, so too does the extent to which the state mandates what is taught in the schools. While some may argue that their state department of education is not mandating at all, other states may require tests of all high school students that cover the topics listed in the state curriculum guide. If the school's test scores are linked to state funding, that is indeed an incentive (even if not required by law) to cover the published curriculum. A state curriculum guide might not say when a curricular topic is supposed to be taught, but if, for example, the mandatory tests for 10th graders consists of algebra and geometry problems, then high schools will certainly organize their classes to teach the algebra and geometry topics covered by that test before the test. Thus, the state curriculum guide is mandating when certain topics are covered, to a certain extent.

Why have the states undertaken the enormous task of "standardizing" the curriculum with their guidelines? The answers vary, but include the argument that having a minimum set of standards will raise the overall quality of education. Legislators want quality and equality in the high schools of their state, so a standards-driven curriculum can be a means to ensure that students in every high school are learning the same things. Have you ever moved from one part of your state to another? Was it hard for you (or for your own children) to adjust to the new school and did you feel behind? Children who have moved a lot during their school careers report that they feel they have been labeled as "gifted" and "brilliant" in some districts, yet were tested for special education services in others! Standards are an attempt to "standardize" as well as to raise quality education. When used at their best, standards can help teachers assess where students are academically in order to better meet their needs.

DISTRICT CURRICULUM

Our country has a long history of local control of schools. Some districts have special topics in their curriculum that are mandated by the district to be taught at certain grade levels. For example, having all ninth graders complete a six-week unit of study on a city's history would be a district mandate that wouldn't necessarily be covered on the state curriculum guide. After all, do all students in Albany need to know the history of Rochester?

A district curriculum guide may take the national standards and the state standards and "flesh them out." If the state standards list the study of colonial literature, the district guidelines may list the book titles to be assigned to all 10th graders. District guidelines may be time specific, as well as inclusive of specific textbooks for each subject. After all, the district is paying for those textbooks, and if a student moves from one high school to another in a district, the curriculum shouldn't change drastically.

A district curriculum guide may be considered a "lifesaver" for a new teacher. It would be very overwhelming to step into a new classroom and simply decide what works of literature 11th graders need to read— or if your class should even be reading novels, as opposed to learning to write every day. Curriculum guides also exist to prevent teachers from simply choosing their favorite topics of the curriculum and teaching them the whole year. A French teacher showed French films almost every week and had students paint pictures of Paris landmarks on the classroom walls. While sophomores in this class could easily discern Notre Dame from the Louvre, few could survive third-year French when they arrived there because they couldn't conjugate verbs. Hence, district curriculum needed to be standardized. (The teacher was fired anyway. Perhaps that teacher didn't understand what was appropriate to teach.)

THE TEXTBOOKS

When asked by a principal to create a curriculum guide for her classes, a new teacher replied, "What do you mean?" The principal replied, "The curriculum is what's in your textbook. Go through your textbook and outline the topics. That's your curriculum." So what did come first, the chicken or the egg? When the standards movement was young, teachers chose textbooks whose topics correlated most closely with the state's published curriculum. Now the textbook publishers have caught up with the movement and have created textbooks built upon the national standards, with special editions for states with specific state guidelines. Some texts were written for the national standards, and have an accompanying CD or website that lists which topics match certain state guidelines—so many states can use the textbook and the teachers can make long-range plans with the supplemental curricular topic data.

States with large student populations have an influence on the curriculum taught in other states. The state of California obviously buys more textbooks than does Wyoming. Publishers will ensure that the curriculum of states buying the largest number of books is included in textbooks so that they can make a sale. Other states sometimes adopt the curriculum of a larger state simply by the use of the same textbook.

As a new teacher, will you get to pick your textbook? The answer is, almost always, "no." You do not have free rein over what materials you use. In many districts a committee of teachers selects the textbooks for a department, and texts are reviewed every five to seven years. In some states, teachers will be asked to select a text from a list of those books approved by the state board of education, and the topics covered in the books on the list match the topics on the state curriculum. Many districts supplement the basic textbooks with readers, workbooks, online materials, and other sources. Many individual teachers also supplement the curriculum with their own choice of books, materials, and activities. However, the choice of a textbook is a significant factor in what gets taught.

NATIONAL AND INTERNATIONAL TESTS

The American College Test (ACT) and Scholastic Aptitude Test (SAT) tests have an influence on the curriculum. Every school in a district wants its ACT and SAT scores to be the highest in the district. These scores are published in the local paper and by the state department of education. Even real estate agents want to know this information so that they can use it in selling houses.

The scores of the states are also published and teachers know where their state stands in the rankings. If a state is near the bottom of the 50 states in the rankings, politicians will use this information to enact reforms. Other politicians will use this information in the next election—perhaps running on the platform that *they* can increase the state's scores and thereby increase the education level of the state's citizens.

The truth is that test scores can be raised with curriculum alignment. Alignment means that the material taught in class is the same material that is tested. If a standardized test contains many vocabulary questions, and those questions are asked in the manner of "nest is to bird" as "_____ is to fox," then test scores will go up if students spend a greater amount of time on vocabulary and learn comparisons in class. Again, textbook publishers are striving to create texts that will help teachers cover the topics on national tests and to provide students practice with the type of testing style used on national tests.

CURRICULUM PLANNING CHECKLIST

In order to have a starting point for your first high school teaching job, you should create a notebook or a file box with some basics about the curriculum. Include the following:

1. The national guidelines for your curriculum. (Most are available online from your professional organization.)
2. The state curriculum guidelines for your subject. (Again, generally available online from your state's department of education. Most students get a list in their curriculum and methods class while in their teacher education program.)
3. A list of current textbooks that are widely used in your field, or gather some sample textbooks.
4. Information about the end-of-course testing or about the state-mandated tests in your subject field.
5. Information about what is on the SAT/ACT tests in your field. (Often a published book about studying for these tests is a good source.)
6. A list of the topics and/or books that you feel are very important to cover in your field.
7. A list of websites for supplemental material.

Once hired, you will need to update your files with:

1. The district's curriculum guide, if used.
2. The building/departmental time line of when topics are taught.
3. A list of books and resources available in your building for supplemental use.

2

PLANNING OF LESSONS, UNITS, AND SYLLABI

In the real world of teaching, you need to gather the curriculum standards and familiarize yourself with them in order to do some long-range planning. As a new teacher in a school, you will probably inherit a "scope and sequence" chart that outlines what your department or curriculum director has determined to be the best plan for covering all the standards in a given semester or year. The scope of the curriculum describes how much content will be covered; the sequence is the order in which it will be taught. If you were to have free rein, you would take the national, state, and district standards, choose a textbook, supplemental activities, and then create your own chart for the scope and sequence of how you would teach your year.

Once you see the big picture of your year, then you can start determining units of study within the curriculum. A unit may be one week to several weeks in length. You can write a unit that helps you to teach the material. A unit plan has broad goals and objectives, specific books or essays to be read, and a variety of activities and assessments of student learning. Many high school teachers write a syllabus for their students for each unit of the school year. A syllabus is a unit plan that contains an explanation of what will be taught, along with "nuts and bolts" details, such as when the tests and quizzes will be given. Planning is something that teachers do to organize the curriculum and to keep themselves on schedule, but sharing the plan with students enables the students to see what they are supposed to be learning and it makes the teaching a lot easier!

With your long-range plans visualized, and a syllabus of two weeks' worth of work outlined for students, you can finally concentrate on an individual lesson plan for teaching one class.

LESSON PLANNING FOR PURPOSEFUL LEARNING

Think back on the best classes you remember from high school. In a class where you learned a lot, and enjoyed the class, do you think that the teacher planned how to present the material? Did he plan activities that reinforced your learning? How did the teacher know if you were learning the material? Did the teacher carry papers around with lesson plans on them? Did she occasionally refer to a plan book with lesson plans written in little boxes about two inches by two inches in size? Did any of your high school teachers use note cards for important information that they were presenting?

Why plan? If you have even the smallest feelings of fear or panic when you imagine facing 28 15-year-olds and keeping them busy and out of trouble for 50 to 90 minutes at a time, then you see the value of planning. When you remember that those same students must not just stay out of trouble in your classroom but also learn the material in their textbook and pass standardized tests, you see the value of planning. *Failing to plan is truly planning to fail.*

LESSON PLAN COMPONENTS

Goals and Objectives

A goal is what the teacher wants to accomplish in a given class. Before you ever step in front of a class, you should know clearly what you intend to do that day with that class. Goals are written with words like present, introduce, model, interpret, read, demonstrate, clarify, and review. Your plan should have one to three goals for each 50- to 90-minute class. Examples include:

Goals for a Spanish lesson
1. The teacher will introduce the typical times for breakfast, lunch, and dinner in Spain.
2. The teacher will show a video of people ordering food in a restaurant in Madrid.
3. The teacher will review all food vocabulary from the video and textbook for chapter 2.

Goals for a math lesson
1. The teacher will review how to find the area of shapes.
2. The teacher will model how to find the circumference of shapes.
3. The teacher will introduce the concept of volume.

Goals for an English lesson
1. The teacher will show a video clip from *Dead Poets' Society* to introduce the value of reading poetry.
2. The teacher will read two of his or her favorite poems.
3. The teacher will introduce vocabulary words for poetry unit, including simile and metaphor.

You will tire quickly of writing "the teacher will" so abbreviate with TTW on your plans.

Objectives

Objectives are what the students should know or be able to *do by the end of the lesson*. It is easy to state objectives in terms of "the student will"; use TSW to save time in planning. An objective must be observable and measurable. In other words, how can you tell that students know or can do what they were supposed to have learned? Some authors of methods textbooks are explicit about objectives, calling them instructional objectives and guiding the teacher to include a specific expected behavior, the conditions under which the student must demonstrate the newly learned behavior and the level of performance expected for each objective (Kellough & Kellough, 1999, p. 201).

Cruikshank, Bainer, and Metcalf (1995) stated that "specific educational objectives give instruction clearer direction in terms of measurable learning outcomes" (p. 139). In the example, "The learner will solve at least eight of ten binary addition problems correctly" (p. 139), it is clear to see that the teacher will be teaching binary addition, and the students will be able to do problems with 80% accuracy.

Gabler and Schroeder (2003) introduce objectives in their methods textbook as "performance objectives" that result in "a physical, digital, or enacted product that your students create" (p. 77). The importance of their definition is that students are doing something with the material presented by the teacher.

Imagine for a moment that you are teaching your subject matter for 180 class sessions. Each session has one to three goals and each goal has one to three objectives. Suddenly, there are 1,620 objectives for each student in your classes to master, and you are teaching four separate class preparations, each with its own set of objectives. Teaching is a complex task—and breaking knowledge down into its most basic components can be a Herculean task. The important thing to remember is that *goals* are what the teacher wants to accomplish and *objectives* are what the students should know or be able to do by the end of the lesson. Objectives may be called instructional objectives, performance objectives, or behavioral objectives (Arends, 1994), but no matter the name, objectives guide us to get students learning and provide us with benchmarks to assess if they have learned what was presented. Goals are what we will cover and objectives are what students will do with what we cover in the lesson.

Here are some sample objectives for a goal of "The teacher will introduce *The Grapes of Wrath* and its characters."

1. The student will be able to name the author of the novel and two facts about his life.
2. TSW be able to identify five important characters in *The Grapes of Wrath*.
3. Given a character from *The Grapes of Wrath*, TSW be able to describe that character with two facts about him or her.

There is obviously so much to teach about any novel, but these objectives start to define what we want students to know about the novel.

As teachers, we simply cannot write "students will read and discuss the book" and think that our classes will go well without detailed directions for the students or for the teacher.

Action verbs for objectives include identify, solve, discuss, list, predict, read, sort, categorize, define, make, create, role-play, and act.

Writing Goals and Objectives

With your state goals in mind, pick a topic that would probably be taught in the grade and subject you are preparing to teach and complete worksheet 2.1.

TEACHING THE LESSON

Resources

With the goals and objectives written for a lesson, you can then identify what resources you will need for the lesson. Obviously, you don't need to write the equipment that is in your classroom every day, like the whiteboard, the overhead, or the TV and VCR. However, you do need to write everything that isn't in your classroom as a reminder that you have to request/procure whatever else you need. You may need to reserve the computer lab or to reserve science lab space. Writing resources also reminds you to remind the students about which textbook, workbook, or outside material they need to bring to class. Science teachers may have a long list of resources on their plan for days in the lab.

Introduction/Focus

Today's students don't just walk into class, organize their desks, and then sit quietly until the bell rings. They do not say or think, "Please teach about NAFTA today in social studies class." Rather, you have to find ways to focus your students on the material every day. The introduction of your class focuses student attention, hooks students on something interesting to motivate them to listen and participate, and also settles them from the chaos of the hallway, lunch, or class just before yours.

Topic: _____

Now write three goals to accomplish with regard to this topic:

1. The teacher will

2. TTW

3.

For each goal, write two objectives for your students to know or do by the end of the lesson.

1. A. The student will

1. B. TSW

2. A.

2. B.

3. A.

3. B.

Worksheet 2.1.   Goals and Objectives

Every day, there should be a spot on your chalkboard/whiteboard or a transparency on an overhead projector that directs the students' attention to a focus activity. Students need to know that every day the routine is the same: they come into the room, they read the focus, and they get busy on it. During the initial few minutes of the class, students should be working while you take attendance silently, without interrupting or wasting any time.

The focus can be called a sponge activity. A sponge activity is defined as any learning activity that "soaks" up time and keeps students busy. These introductory activities are not just busy work, but should pique the students' interest and get them thinking about your subject. They can be review questions or anticipatory questions. Examples include:

Social studies: When introducing trade agreements, or how the United States trades with foreign nations, ask students to make a list of any product that they have on them or with them that was not made in America. Students go through their backpacks and purses, check the labels on their clothes, and make a list of what was made where. (This could be a noisy activity, as students need help to read the labels in their shirts, but noise is OK if it is on-task.) After attendance, the class generates a list of articles made in other countries.

English: The students will be asked to write about moving. Have you ever moved? If yes, write about how you felt when your family moved. If you have never moved, write about how you would feel if you went home tonight and your family announced that you were moving to a new state 1,000 miles away. This settling activity promotes student thinking about the experience of moving and can be an introduction to *The Grapes of Wrath*.

Science: The focus on the board asks students to get out one piece of paper and number it 1 through 6, allowing three lines of space in between numbers. When the bell rings, you show a video of a science experiment and students write the six most important steps that they see on the video. Depending on the experiment shown, students may replicate that same experiment later in the lab, or the video of the experiment may promote discussion. (Students love it when their science teacher has made the video!)

Math: The easiest way to focus student attention is to involve them in problem solving. The focus may be a homework problem or a new question that will introduce the new lesson.

Do you grade the sponge/focus activity, and if so, how do you grade it? If you don't grade it, will students even bother to do it? Some teachers never grade the sponge but insist that students copy the sponge into their notebooks because the same questions that appear on the board will constitute a portion of the test questions. Students know that they need to do the sponge and that the answers will help them do better on the unit tests. Some teachers grade the sponge occasionally but do not tell students when it will be picked up for a grade. Grading even one sponge every two weeks motivates students to do it, and grading the answer to one problem is not very time consuming.

Madeline Hunter (1994) called the introduction to a lesson the "anticipatory set" and suggested that it be used to focus the student's attention on the planned objectives.

"Anticipatory set" results from a brief activity that occurs at the beginning of the lesson or when students are mentally "shifting" gears from one activity to the next. The purpose of the anticipatory set is to elicit students' attending behavior, focus them on the content of the ensuing instruction, and develop a mental readiness (or "set") for it. (Hunter, 1994, p. 95)

Sometimes the introduction can be fun, too. Imagine if students come to social studies class and are anxious to talk about the recent presidential election. Have students write three things that they have heard on the television news about the election and start teaching from what the students already know and want to discuss. In math, have the students calculate the chances of the team winning the next big game, based on the team's past record. It's statistics *and* it's meaningful to them.

Body of the Lesson

Variety is the key to the body of the lesson. The lesson should be a combination of the teacher presenting new material and the students actively engaging in learning experiences. You will present new material by giving modified lectures (keep them shorter than 12 minutes for high school students), giving demonstrations, showing videos, and using the Internet. After you present new material, students need to do something with the material, like discuss it, make their own model, problem-solve, read, write, or answer questions. If you are teaching on a block schedule with 70 to 90 minutes, you will have cycles of presentation, activities, presentation, and activities. Hands-on activities are very good, but in high school we are especially concerned that the body of the lesson be "minds-on" for the students. If students are not thinking and doing something with the material, they won't be learning it.

Within the seven elements of Madeline Hunter's lesson design, she devoted much time to instructional input, modeling, and guided practice (1994). Instructional input is actual teaching and so is modeling. For example, a math teacher models the best way to solve a problem or to prove a theorem and then the students do problems as the teacher walks around and checks their work (guided practice). Students need a lot of practice in order to make their learning automatic. Imagine learning French in high school. Being told by the teacher that "pain" is the word for bread may not mean that you remember that word or can use it in a sentence. Watching a video of teenagers in Dijon, France, ordering lunches from McDonald's doesn't mean that you can order lunch from McDonald's when you go to Dijon. However, the video and the teacher's use of the language start your learning of the language. You must practice diligently to master the material. Reading a dialogue in French with two partners will help you practice. Writing a dialogue for you and a fast-food counter worker will enhance your learning. Taking a quiz on food vocabulary will prompt you to study. This is what is meant by hands-on, minds-on, active learning. It is guided practice because the teacher is there to correct, monitor, and explain the more challenging aspects of the lesson. All of this takes place in the body of the lesson.

Conclusion

Of course, a lesson needs a conclusion because everything needs some sort of closure. The conclusion to a lesson can do several things—provide assessment information on what the students have learned that day, help the teacher know where to begin the next day, and motivate the students to look forward to returning to class. Quizzes, both graded and ungraded, are one way to assess individual student learning at the end of a lesson. Asking questions and listening to students' responses will give the teacher a way to assess what students have learned. Some teachers have students write out the answer to one question on a slip of paper as a ticket to leave class. The teacher can read the answers while standing at the door and see if students have learned.

The conclusion to a class certainly does not have to be teacher-led and shouldn't be led by the teacher every day. Have students tell what they learned or what was the most interesting fact presented during the class. When a history teacher tells about the Pacific Campaign during World War II, students should be able to tell a fact that they learned that surprised them about this difficult period of U.S. history. In fact, the sponge activity for that lesson might have been, "Write something you know about the war in the Pacific during World War II (WWII) and listen for the most surprising fact that will be your ticket at the door at the end of class."

A key to student learning is tying the lesson together from the beginning to the end. A high school teacher should always post in writing what the students will learn during the class. In states with a strictly mandated curriculum, teachers may write the state's curriculum topic on the board for each day. Some teachers phrase what students will learn as an essential question, such as "How does the reader find meaning in a poem?" and then students are expected to be able to answer all the essential questions on the unit test. An advantage of this is that if students copy the topics or questions from the board each day, then they automatically know what is on the test. Should students know what will be asked on tests? Absolutely they should. If they know what they are supposed to learn and don't learn it, who is responsible? They are, and we want them to take responsibility for their own learning. In this age of accountability, we also want to demonstrate to principals and parents that we have organized our teaching in order to facilitate the students' learning. Essential questions and topic outlines of the day's work hold the students responsible.

Adaptations for Lesson

Students with exceptionalities will be in your high school classes. Exceptionalities may include learning disabilities, physical handicaps, and language minority status or limited English proficiency. Don't forget that exceptionally gifted and talented students will be in your classes and adaptations should be made to enhance their learning as well. Winebrenner (1992) wrote that it is the most able students "who will learn less material than any other group" (p. 1). So, adaptations of your basic lesson plan need to be considered in order for the lesson to be appropriate for all students.

Adaptations may be as simple as moving some students closer to the screen when you use the overhead projector. An adaptation may be having two worksheets—one with no vocabulary definitions and one with definitions included. Writing an outline of the material you plan to say may be an asset to give to a special education teacher who will work with one or more of your students later in the day. Having a plan for accommodating students who will take 50 minutes to complete a quiz and those who will take 20 minutes is an adaptation. Planning ahead and writing a reminder on your lesson plan will help the students who need individualized attention and it should help your class flow more smoothly.

Speculation

Teachers with years of experience generally don't write down a speculation, but they do think about how the lesson will go. Even veteran teachers wonder how students will react to a new activity, and all teachers question themselves about the factor of time. When you are teaching a lesson for the first time, try writing at least two questions about the lesson, such as "Will this material fit into one class session?" and "How many students will be able to do the advanced problems?" Asking speculative questions will also guide you to some of the adaptations and may force you to add an "extra" activity or set of questions to the body of the lesson so that you feel more prepared.

Reflection

Many teachers don't write a formal reflection after they teach each lesson. Often, there is simply no time to do this in a busy high school setting. However, reflecting on how a lesson went and what the teacher might be able to change are very important ideas. If nothing else, write down a phrase or two as a reminder for the next time you teach the lesson. You might remind yourself to allow more time to discuss the video that introduced the lesson, since students had a lot of questions. You may write a note to leave two questions off of the review sheet, since they were simply too difficult for students at this point in the unit.

In the real world of teaching, effective teachers put notes in their plan books as reminders for the next year. Sometimes we don't even need to wait that long to change a lesson, as we may be teaching another section of the same class later in the day.

The essential question of "Why write a lesson plan?" has probably been answered for you by this section of the book. Lesson planning helps keep the teacher on track and organizes the curriculum into teachable "chunks." Good lesson planning is shared with the students so that they know what they are supposed to be doing. Preparation is the key and there really is no such thing as being overprepared for high school teaching!

Lesson Planning Review

- Teaching should always be purposeful.
- Teaching must be meaningful for the student.
- Goals and objectives (based on national, state, district curriculum?)
    1. *Goals:* What the teacher wants to accomplish (present, introduce, model, interpret, read, demonstrate).
    2. *Objectives:* What the students will know or be able to do by the end of the lesson (identify, solve, discuss, list, predict, read, sort, categorize, define, make, create, role-play, act).
- Resources for lesson: Books? Technology? Pens? Paper? Demonstration materials?
- Introduction = Focus
  Hook the students on the lesson to be presented. Connect what will be learned to what students already know. Let students know what they will learn. Present a problem or dilemma that would lead to further study. Settle class and get their attention.
- Body of lesson
    - teacher presents new material
    - students participate in guided practice of new material and/or
    - students explore and complete activity with the new material
    - teacher makes ongoing assessment of students' learning
    - teacher may review and provide more practice or activities

- teacher may start cycle of presentation, guided student practice, activities, and assessment over with new material
- Conclusion
  - assess student learning
  - provide closure to this class while relating what was learned with what will be learned in the future
  - keep students actively involved in conclusion; they can restate what they learned and why it's important
- Adaptations of lesson:
  - What special considerations are needed for students with exceptionalities? (desks moved? different vocabulary? consultation with special ed teacher?)
  - What needs to be planned for gifted students and those who finish early?
- Speculation:
  - Will students be able to learn this material and complete the practice and activities in the time provided?
  - Will they find this lesson interesting?
  - What fears do you have about this lesson? What needs to be practiced before you present to the students?
- Reflection:
  - How did this lesson go? (time, student behavior, interest, amount of learning)
  - What would you change if you were to teach this lesson again?

Remember:

Goals
Objectives
Resources
Introduction
Body
Conclusion
Adaptations
Speculation
Reflection

See worksheet 2.2 for a lesson plan template.

Class: _____

Date: _____

Topic(s): _____

State standard(s) met: _____

Goals

1. TTW
2. TTW

Objectives: (each goal must have an objective)

1. TSW
2. TSW
3. TSW

Resources for lesson:

Introduction = Focus

- TTW
- TSW

Body of lesson

- TTW
- TSW

Conclusion (include assessment of student learning)

Adaptations of lesson:

Speculation:

Reflection: (Written after the lesson is taught; think about what you and the students will do next time)

Worksheet 2.2. Lesson Plan Template

UNITS OF STUDY

What Are Units?

When you look at the state's curriculum standards or the district's curriculum guide for your subject, it is important to ask, "How does all of this fit together?" How long will you spend on each topic? Will the book be the major resource used to teach each topic? How can topics be grouped together? Will you be teaching each topic by yourself, or will teams of teachers coplan and coteach some topics? The answer to these questions is that you need to create "chunks" of teaching material and these chunks are units of study.

When you are given a textbook, it is easy to look at the chapters and then say, "OK, the units are planned for me by the chapters of the book." This, however, is not necessarily the best way to plan a unit. The material in the book's chapter may not align completely with your district and state goals. Many book chapters have no projects or activities, just readings, and having students read every day lacks variety. So, while a well-written textbook chapter may be the primary source of material for a unit of study, the chapter does not constitute a unit.

Just as a principal will ask you to turn in your lesson plans, you may also be asked to turn in unit plans. In some schools, these plans are defined as three lines about the topics to be covered for each day of the length of the unit. So, in the simplest form, a unit of study is a list of dates for two to three weeks, with topics, page numbers from the text, homework assignments, and test dates. However, this could also be considered a calendar.

A well-thought-out unit plan actually looks much like a lesson plan, but a unit plan is for several days or weeks, not just a 50- to 90-minute lesson. A unit has a topic or theme. A thematic unit is one that is focused on just one area, such as colonization in a survey course in American history. An integrated unit is one where the subject-matter boundaries are blurred. For example, if a class of ninth graders studies colonization in history class and reads literature from the period in literature, then there exists the opportunity for the two teachers to combine their work into one unit. There may be just one test that counts for both classes. The teachers may share their class time and team-teach. They may work together with the students on one culminating activity (the staging of a play from the time period) and can certainly share a guest speaker.

Even if teachers are working alone on their units, they should share some of the points of the plan with other faculty. Unit tests should not be the same day in three high school subjects, major papers should not be due at the same time in a nine-week grading period, and sometimes teachers do have to consider the timing of homecoming and athletic events in their long-range planning.

So, if you are planning a unit, start with the topic/theme. Decide how long you will need to teach this unit and where it best fits in the semester. When planning a unit of at least 10 days, allow a catch-up day the first time you teach the unit. Remember that student attendance is often sporadic, and we want as many students as possible to master the material presented before a unit test/assessment.

Why are you teaching this unit anyway? Is it vitally important that students know this material? The *philosophy* behind your unit is important. Not only should you have a philosophy for the importance of the unit but you should also share this philosophy with the students. In essence, you have to sell the importance of the unit to your students, because they don't arrive at your classroom, sit down, look at the front of the room, and say, "Oh, please teach us the importance of the industrial revolution."

Knowing the philosophy of the unit will enable you to write clear unit goals and objectives. Again, the goals are what the teacher will do. Unit goals might include:

- TTW introduce the history of the decade before the United States entered WWII.
- TTW outline the major historical battles of WWII.
- TTW generate discussion of the effects of WWII on the United States after 1946.
- TTW bring speakers to the class who describe the war or the times of the 1940s.

Each goal in a unit will have several student objectives, since students may be working on these objectives over several days. Objectives for the above goals might include:

- TSW be able to write about three events of historical significance that lead up to WWII.

- TSW make a timeline of WWII with at least 20 significant dates and events.
- TSW generate a list of five questions to ask a veteran of the war and five questions to ask a person who was alive but in the United States during the war years.

Learning Experiences in a Unit

Learning experiences are what students do in order to meet the objectives of the unit. Obviously, students can read their textbook and supplemental sources and then discuss what they read. Students can view a video and then create a set of questions they would have asked if they were producing the show. Students can make individual timelines and then create a timeline large enough to hold the events that everyone put on their small timeline, showing the extent of the era studied. Continuing the WWII example, students could show the war years in terms of months, making each month five-feet long on the time line, and then hanging the completed project in the gym or hallway to emphasize the length of the war. A research project that integrates math into the unit might include making a chart of how many total deaths occurred from 1940 to 1948 that were attributable to the war. Again, displayed on a wall, this can be staggering information. A second group of students can make a graph comparing deaths in WWII to those in WWI, the Korean conflict, Vietnam, and the Gulf War.

Learning experiences can include work both inside and outside of the classroom. Students can visit a local VFW chapter and hear a speaker or interview veterans. They can visit a local war monument or memorial. Chapters 3 through 5 of this book on methods elaborate on ways of teaching and learning, but the important thing to remember is that students participate in learning activities to meet planned objectives. Listening to a good lecture in class and taking notes can be a valid learning experience as well.

Assessment of the Unit

The most conventional way of determining if students have mastered the objectives of a unit has been to give a test over the material covered. Tests are indeed one way of assessing learning. Students' papers, essays, projects, group presentations, portfolios, and computer assignments are also ways to verify that students are learning. Assessment and grading are separate issues, and are discussed later in this book (see chapter 7).

We assess throughout the teaching of the unit to determine if students are learning the material at the pace presented. This ongoing assessment is formative and may or may not be graded. Formative assessments help the teacher determine the scope and content of individual lesson plans. Assessments at the end of the unit are summative ones and are usually graded.

Resources to Teach a Unit

The textbook is one resource, and still the most common one. Some resources must be ordered in advance, such as videos. Guest speakers, even if they are teachers down the hall, can require a lot of planning, but may be well worth the effort. Don't overlook Internet resources, other teachers' experience, and your own experience. Field trips can make the unit come alive.

Review for Creating a Unit Plan

- Grade level for this unit:
- Topic(s)
- Length of time needed to teach unit, place in semester
- Philosophy
  - Why is this unit important?
  - How does it relate to previous or future work?
  - How does impact students' experiences and current lives?
  - Why do we teach this?
- Goals and objectives. What the teacher will do. For example,
  - Goal 1. To present information about unit planning.
  - Goal 2. To demonstrate how a unit is different from a syllabus.
  - Goal 3. To show students the link between lesson planning and unit planning.

- Objectives
  - TSW write an acceptable unit plan on poster paper by the end of the class.
  - TSW be able to identify the parts of a unit plan.
  - TSW will be able to differentiate the differences between unit plans, lesson plans, and a syllabus.
- Learning experiences
  - What can students do to learn the material needed to meet the objectives?
  - What will the teacher present?
  - Describe these experiences.
- Assessment: Tests, portfolios, papers, essays, group presentations, computer assignments, etc.
  - How can you assess if they met the objectives?
  - Is your assessment formative or cumulative?
- Resources
  - What do you need to implement this unit?
  - Can you bring in speakers?
  - Use computers?
  - Which books will the students have?
  - Which book will you have?

See worksheet 2.3 for a unit plan template.

USING A SYLLABUS

While a unit plan creates organization for the teacher, a syllabus shares the "nuts and bolts" of what will be done in class with the student. Every teacher remembers how college professors gave a syllabus to students on the first day of class and followed it throughout the semester. A syllabus for high school students will not cover an entire semester because that might totally overwhelm students. Also, high schools have more interruptions than colleges and a semester-long syllabus would need a myriad of changes. At the high school level, a syllabus works well when prepared for each unit of study. Students can use a two- to four-week syllabus to plan their study time and get themselves organized. Again, if students know in

Grade level for this unit:

Topic(s):

Length of time needed to teach unit, place in semester:

Philosophy:

Objectives:
1.

2.

3.

Learning experiences:

Assessment:

Resources:

Worksheet 2.3.   The Unit Plan Template

advance when assignments are due, then they are responsible for doing them. Parents and administrators appreciate the organization of a teacher who provides a clear syllabus to students.

A syllabus is for students, so it should include a unit description that tells them why they need to know the material. If possible, make the unit description really exciting! Students need to know what materials they need to bring to class, so include that information. Telling students your goals will help them to understand what you are doing, and obviously the objectives tell them what they will learn.

The calendar is quite important. While you need to work around the big events of the high school social calendar, it is impossible to plan due dates and test dates that are at convenient times for everyone. By letting students know the critical dates ahead of time, they are held responsible for their own time management. In real life we are held accountable to due dates also. The calendar should include topics, readings, and homework. High school students have actually told their teachers that one reason they skip class is because "we knew that we wouldn't do anything anyway." If every day has a topic, a reading, and an activity, students know that they will do something.

Students should also know in advance what will be involved in completing the major projects, papers, and assignments. Tell them this in the section for assessment criteria. Share as much as possible about how they will be graded and how they can earn the maximum number of points. Include rubrics for the activities and projects. (The design of assessment and rubrics is covered in chapter 7.)

Review of Syllabus Writing

- Course name
- Instructor's name
- Semester or nine weeks
- Instructor's e-mail
- Course or unit description
- In high school teaching, a unit will be two to four weeks. Describe the unit within the course and the rationale or philosophy for teaching this. When students ask, "Why is this important?" this paragraph tells them.

- Materials required by student
  Include the name of a text, if possible, and other materials or special supplies.
- Goals
  Just like on your other plans, these are the teacher's goals of introducing, presenting, and so forth.
- Objectives
  Every goal should one to three specific student objectives. (TSW . . .)
- Calendar with assignments
  Class #1, Monday   Include a topic for each day, homework, and assignments. Highlight a test or project.
  Continue with all classes in the unit, remembering to add one catch-up day.
- Assessment criteria
  For at least three of the major items to be graded from the above calendar, describe the test, activity, or project with a short paragraph.
- Grading scales and rubrics for the unit and the individual assessment pieces

3

METHODS FOR TEACHER
PRESENTATIONS

When writing about how to teach in *The Courage to Teach*, Parker J. Palmer (1998) explained that "Technique is what teachers use until the real teacher arrives" (p. 5). Some people believe that teachers are born with innate, natural talents to stand up in front of the class and deliver the subject matter to students. Others believe that teacher candidates can be taught a set of teaching skills that will enable them to present material in meaningful ways. Palmer's quote indicates that teachers need techniques (methods) to rely on until their teaching becomes innate, second nature, and part of who they are and what they do.

Now that you know where the curriculum comes from and how to organize it into lessons and units, it is time to learn how to teach it. If curriculum is *what* we teach, then methods are *how* we teach. Even so-called natural teachers can improve on their skills with knowledge of strategies for presenting material and engaging students in learning.

GET TO KNOW WHAT STUDENTS KNOW

A college professor of mine said that you can't teach students until you know what they know and what interests them. Learning is a building process, and a foundation has to be in place before floors can be added to a building. My professor said to begin lessons on new topics with "APIK" activities—ones that assess prior interest and knowledge. Gabler and Schroeder (2003) call this method "ILPE," which represents "investigating learners' previous experiences" (p. 222).

At the beginning of a school year or semester, do not assume that your students know the background needed to learn your subject. Even if you see the curriculum guide used by the previous grade, do not assume that all students learned the material presented in the guide. While curriculum should have vertical alignment (the topics in one grade are sequenced with the topics taught before and after), alignment does not mean that students remember all the facts with each topic—yet it is impossible to reteach all the previous material that students should know. Where should a teacher start?

Questioning and pretesting are good ways to find out what students know and remember from previous classes. At the beginning of the new year, pretest students in a nonthreatening way with some ungraded tests, essays, and discussions. "Ungraded" here means that you assess the test, but the score is not used in determining the student's semester grade. Math and science teachers can create tests by examining the material in their first units of study, then writing a test of what students need to know before starting the unit. If the pretests are low, a few days of work may be needed to get the group caught up. This is a much better way to start a semester than teaching a unit and having 75% of the students fail the first graded test because they didn't have the academic background needed to even start the lesson.

English teachers often have students write on the first days of class in order to assess their skills. A nongraded writing sample can tell the teacher much about students' former learning. Be careful not to judge the students' former teachers by these early assessments. I used to give nongraded review tests to returning students in my foreign language classes and sometimes could hardly believe how much they forgot over the summer—and I had been their previous teacher!

Discussions can provide insight into students' prior knowledge and their ability to make rational arguments. Verbal skills are assessable through discussion, as are students' participation skills. (See chapter 4 for a section on teaching with questions to plan a lesson using questions to assess prior knowledge.)

How interested are students in your subject matter? It was John Dewey who said that education was rooted in experience of the learner (Dewey, 1998). When you first meet your new students, you need to learn their backgrounds and interests. The interest inventories that you give to students the first week of school will help you to accomplish this (see chapter 8 for more information on interest inventories). If a student completes an interest inventory telling you that her goals include medical school, you can estimate that her interest in biology is quite high. What about the student who writes that his goal is to become an interpreter at the United Nations and that he hates science? How can you use his past negative interest to motivate him to learn biology? What would your reaction be to a 16-year-old who said chemistry interested him because of wanting to be a drug dealer? Remember that students will sometimes tell you more than you really want to know and that you are responsible to take their information to trained counselors in the schools for help in dealing with them.

GET TO KNOW HOW STUDENTS LEARN

Stop and ask yourself the following questions:

1. How do I learn best?
2. Do I like to hear the information first, then see a visual?
3. Do I always need to see a picture?
4. Do I like hands-on activities?
5. Do I learn better when I can create a drawing or model of the subject matter?
6. In which classes did I have trouble learning the material? Why?
7. What could my teachers have done to help me learn the material better?
8. Did I always have enough time to complete assignments and tests?
9. Did I learn much from discussions?
10. Did I ever feel that my talents/creativity were simply suppressed by the teacher? Why?

Now create a worksheet with similar questions to ask your students about their learning styles. Be sure and include some questions that are specific to your field. These might include:

- You have studied World War II at several stages in elementary and middle school. List five facts you know about the war and one activity or lesson that a teacher presented that helped you learn this material.
- Write a paragraph in German about high school. What do you like? Dislike? What are your favorite foods? What do you do in your free time?
- Math teachers can include three to five problems for students to solve, then ask students how they learned to solve those problems. Ask them to describe their process of attacking any math problem.
- English teachers often ask students to write two to three short paragraphs about their favorite book. Make the assignment more personal by asking students to write the paragraphs to the audience of the English department about why they should assign this book to every student.
- Examples vary for science, depending on the field. You can ask students to write about a current event and how science played a role in that event. Asking specific questions or how to set up an experiment will also give you insight into their knowledge and interest.

Howard Gardner's work on multiple intelligences (Campbell, 1994) has changed how many teachers plan their teaching because it has made teachers aware of how students learn and process information. Later works on learning styles and learning modalities have further enabled teachers to identify how students prefer to learn and can therefore match teaching styles with learning styles. It is essential to remember that many students are visual—they must see a picture or cue to learn material. Many students are tactile and need to touch and feel manipulatives in order to comprehend. Others are very kinesthetic and need to move around a lot during a lesson, perhaps learning better to a mnemonic that is hummed or to a rap that they can perform. Yet, for years, high school teachers were guilty of just talking to teach, and that style only recognizes the auditory skills of students.

Finding out how students learn is a course of study in and of itself—that's why educational psychology classes are included in teacher education programs. As a teacher, remember to introduce new material in a variety of ways to reach all the learners in your class.

ROLE OF TEXTBOOKS AND RESOURCES

Many college professors have been heard to say, "Throw away the textbook and actually teach." Many student teachers have been terrified by these words. I have told my own student teachers, "Find the very best textbook you can, and use it as a resource." There is no reason to reinvent the wheel. There are some very good textbooks that include excellent examples and clear summaries of the knowledge base you are teaching. In fact, if possible, create a library of textbooks, new and old, in your classroom or department. Use them when your students need extra drills, readings, and practice. Of course, be careful that old textbooks contain correct information. The geography of the world has changed dramatically since the 1980s and scientific theories change our view of science constantly. However, some classic literature texts simply do not go out of style.

As you implement the following teaching methods and strategies, your textbook can serve as a resource for all of the methods. Although teaching with the Internet and other technology can be considered a method of teaching, the Internet and technology are also resources for some of the other methods. Guest speakers, newspapers, magazines, primary sources, and pieces of artwork are also teaching resources. As a teacher, you will be building files of materials to teach your subject. Use everything you can get your hands on to enhance student learning and raise student achievement.

METHOD 1: THE LECTURE/PRESENTATION

Why did your college professors give lectures? Why did your high school teachers give lengthy presentations? Why do teachers talk? The lecture/presentation method of teaching has a long history in education. Simply put, a lecture is a means to give a lot of information to a large number of students in a short amount of time. College professors give lectures when they have halls filled with hundreds of students. High school teachers give lectures because they are experts in their fields and have a lot of material to convey to students and a limited amount of time. Also, high school teachers are held accountable for the thousands of topics and facts that will all be on the end-of-course standardized test. Sometimes an instructor will tell a story so mesmerizing that all the students will remember it—and learn from it. Yes, there are advantages to giving a lecture.

There are also disadvantages. Walker (1998) wrote that "Less than 30% of the students in classrooms learn by lecture" (p. 1). Lecturing every day and not letting the students respond, ask questions, discuss, or practice the new material simply will not work in today's high schools. Since time, money, and history imply that we will continue presenting new material in this way, the best approach to lecturing is to create an enhanced lecture. In other words, let's make the lecture a good one that works!

Callahan, Clark, and Kellough (1998) remind teachers that we talk too much and too fast. In fact, some teachers talk without considering if they are even being heard or understood. Worse yet, some teachers forget that hearing doesn't necessarily mean understanding or learning on the part of the student. What can a teacher do to make a lecture or presentation more useful as a learning tool for students?

1. Be visual. At the very least, make sure that students can see the main points of the lecture/presentation on a screen. You can project onto the screen with an overhead projector or computer-generated presentation. While some teachers still write on the board, prepared overheads or PowerPoint slides can be used over and over again. In order for students to see what is on the screen, remember to use no font smaller than 24 point and to limit notes on the screen to three ideas at a time. Also, any notes created with word processing can be spell-checked. Many teachers need to spell-check work before it is shown and some teachers do not write legibly on a board. Writing on a board also implies that your back is turned to the students, something that we don't want to do in many classrooms for management reasons.

2. Be visual with pictures you bring in from the media center, local library, or other sources. If your room has online access, show students websites with pictures that support your lecture. Again, project these pictures onto a big screen so that students can see the material clearly. Today's high school students attend concerts where the "star" performs and is seen on huge screens around the concert hall. Let's learn from this and take advantage of what performers have learned about capturing the attention of the audience! For example, when lecturing on how cells reproduce, a biology teacher can also show *cellsalive* on the screen from www.cellsalive.com. A history teacher can lecture about the Civil War, then go to www.confederatemuseum.com to show pictures of uniforms, weapons, and so forth. Math teachers can liven up their lectures about Pascal's triangle by showing http://ptri1.tripod.com as they talk.

3. Be visual by keeping the objectives for the lesson on the board or on a flip chart that students can refer to as you talk and use the screen.

4. Your lecture will be more interesting with advance organizers that capture the students' attention. Try something different—maybe reading from a novel to introduce the anguish felt by individuals who have sent their spouses off to war.

5. Your lecture, which should only be 10 to 12 minutes before breaking for questions and activities, should always have an introduction, a body, and a conclusion.

6. Remember to use the rules that you learned for public speaking in your speech communications classes: make eye contact, vary the tone in your voice, show excitement and animation, and monitor the students' body language.

7. Unlike public speaking from behind a podium, *move around*! Some students will listen only when they think that you are staring at them or are a foot away. If you use notes or technology, carry the notes or use a remote.

Bonwell and Eison (1991) recommend giving what they call "modified lectures." A modified lecture is short, 12 to 18 minutes, and then has a break for questions to and from students. A lecture can have built-in breaks for discussion, even in a large classroom. The instructor can talk for 10 minutes, then say, "Turn to the person on your right and compare notes. In 60 seconds I will ask for four students to each share a major cause of the current Middle East conflict. Go." Another catchy idea is to ask students to *write nothing* for five minutes, then stop lecturing and ask students to write the three most important points made by the instructor. After students write, the instructor then reveals the points on the big screen.

If classroom space permits, have students listen to your lecture, then have half of the room write down "pros" of the debate from the lecture on one side of the room and "cons" on the board on the other side of the room.

If you lecture, you must make sure that students are learning from your lecture. Have students write a one-minute paper at the end of your class to assess their learning. This type of paper generally has just two questions: "What was the clearest point of my talk today?" and "What was the most unclear point?" You can make this paper graded or un-graded or just collect for a two-point participation grade. Some instructors make the review paper anonymous—they truly just want the feedback from the learners. The one-minute summary paper can also be topic specific. For example, ask two questions about what you taught. Examples might include, "How can our government prevent another Great Depression from occurring today?" or "How can we stop the spread of new diseases like SARS?" The students' answers will provide feedback about where you should start teaching tomorrow.

A final reminder about teaching with a lecture is that you do know more than your students about the subject matter and you should share your personal expertise with them. However, students have learned to *not* listen at an early age, and a lecture without visuals is just teacher talk. To make the lecture work, it must be organized and it must be supported with visuals. Presentations should be short with questions, answers, and active learning interspersed throughout the talking. Unfortunately, we can't just take a big cup, scoop knowledge up from our brains, and pour it into our students' minds. They have to hear our knowledge, see a representation of it, and then do something with the knowledge to make it their own.

METHOD 2: CONCEPT ATTAINMENT

An integral part of teaching any subject matter is the teaching of concepts. A concept is an idea, a thought, a theory, an abstraction, or a view. "Equality" is a concept taught one way by math teachers and another way by teachers of government and history. Science teachers teach complex concepts—light, matter, gravity, propulsion, and so on. The concepts of paragraph, verb tense, and genre may take days or weeks to teach to an English class. We break concepts down and make them "learnable" for the student by the following:

1. *Definitions.* We often simplify material for students by trying to define terms. When new concepts are introduced, we must provide definitions. The same rules that we used for lecturing hold for presenting definitions. Be visual. Write definitions clearly and project them for students to see. Make sure students are taking notes. As we define concepts, we should share characteristics, so that students gain a clearer understanding.

2. *Examples and non-examples.* We often teach concepts by providing examples and non-examples. After the teacher models a few clear examples and non-examples, then students can discuss and debate other examples. Examples: These are classic poems. These are not poems at all, but short prose examples. Then the teacher shares very modern examples of poetry and asks for student input. Perhaps the teacher started the poetry unit with clear examples of poems that use similes and metaphors, then gave poems that had neither. Are these still poems? Why or why not? Every art teacher has led multiple discussions of "What is art?" and biology teachers spend a long time on "What is life?"

These examples of teaching concepts by teaching definitions, vocabulary, examples, and non-examples seem very teacher centered, with the teacher providing the new information as facts. The teaching of concepts can be done deductively or inductively; as with any teaching method or strategy, knowing your students and their backgrounds will help you decide when to use which strategy.

"Deductive teaching is defined as a style of teaching in which the instructor presents the class with one or more concepts or principles, challenges students to investigate a set of examples that are related to these main ideas, and then asks the students to test or apply the central ideas" (Gabler & Schroeder, 2003, p. 122). When teaching concepts deductively, the teacher presents the concept with a definition, vocabulary, and examples, and then directs students to explore the concept further. Math teachers often do this with a new concept, and the problem solving that ensues is the application of the new material. An English teacher who presents the rules for writing a persuasive essay and then has students read several and write their own original one is also teaching a concept deductively.

Teaching concepts *inductively* is sometimes called discovery teaching, since the teacher does not begin with a name for a concept or with definitions and clear examples. A teacher who asks students to read several essays and then asks what all have in common is teaching the concept of the essay inductively. A science teacher who gives a demonstration and then asks, "Why?" is doing the same thing. Why should teachers vary their approach? Some students want to have their learning guided from the most basic of concrete ideas to the more abstract. They want to learn a new idea and then play with it. Other students want to discover things on their own and then figure out the why. My husband tells a story of taking apart the family's toaster when he was just four years old. When his mother discovered him with the toaster in pieces she immediately asked, "What on earth are you doing?" His reply was simple, "I want to know how it works." Being four, he didn't have a clue about reading a schematic diagram to see how it worked, but he knew he could take it apart and find out. Students with this learning style should be encouraged, or at least not discouraged, in our classes. After all, four-year-olds who can take toasters apart can turn out to be terrific engineers, as my husband did. Disassembling and reassembling abstract concepts, as well as things, help students learn, and discovering the concept may hold the interest of some students. If the inductive approach is too frustrating for some, make an adaptation for them, like a hint sheet with some vocabulary. Use both approaches to keep students thinking (see worksheet 3.1).

Think of 10 commonly taught concepts in your field. Although commonly taught, they should also be higher-order concepts that need more than a few minutes to teach.

1. List the most challenging of the 10 concepts to teach.

2. Define this concept.

3. List three to five vocabulary words associated with this concept that should be taught simultaneously.

4. List three basic characteristics of this concept.

5. Examples of this concept include

   1.
   2.
   3.

   Non-examples of this concept include

   1.
   2.
   3.

6. This concept is important because

7. This concept is tied to previous learning through

Worksheet 3.1.   Planning a Concept Attainment Lesson

METHOD 3: USE OF GRAPHIC ORGANIZERS

It may well be true that "a picture is worth a thousand words." When students can make their own pictures, the value of the picture may well be worth 10,000 words. Graphic organizers help teachers to present information and help students to organize and learn that information. A graphic organizer can be as simple as a circle with a topic written in it. Lines to other circles with ideas that the students believe are related can be added. Called a web, teaching with a graphic like this on the board or a large sheet of poster paper can help students brainstorm about what fiction is. You may give the class a handout with one circle and 15 surrounding ones to generate ideas for how to achieve peace in a specific region of the world. The center circle might be filled with the protagonist of a novel and each circle around it represents a character and how they are related to the main character. Little lines make the web complete as one subcharacter relates to other subcharacters (see figure 3.1). Give this handout to students before they read the novel and have them fill in the blank circles each time a new character appears.

There are two important questions with regard to graphic organizers. The first is what the teacher will do with the organizer. Will the teacher draw it on the board or show it on an overhead for students to copy as a presentation is being made? Will the teacher fill it in with student-generated ideas or present it as a completed organizer with "facts" in each box or circle? The second question covers what the student will do with the organizer. If the teacher is doing all the work with the organizer, it is only as useful as showing any picture. When the students start using the organizer, then their learning is more active.

The KWL Chart

The KWL chart graphic organizer is a great tool for introducing new material, assessing student knowledge, finding out what students want to learn about the subject, and then reviewing at the end of the lesson or unit (see worksheet 3.2).

Teachers, as curriculum designers, often forget that students may already know a lot about a topic. Students may think that they know things that are false assumptions as well. A KWL chart addresses former knowl-

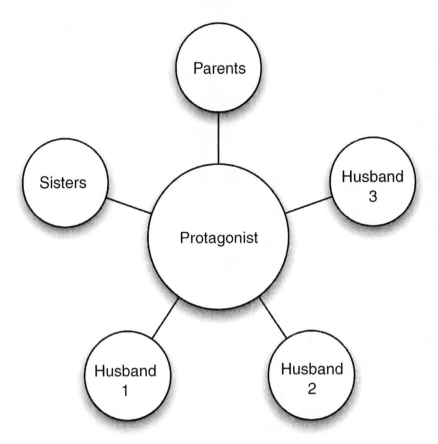

Figure 3.1.   Sample Web

edge and false assumptions. For example, when studying the 1960s, students may know quite a bit about that era. They may be able to generate
facts for the "what I know" column about the Vietnam War, the War on
Poverty, school desegregation, bell-bottom pants, and so forth. When
asked about the presidency, they may list false assumptions, thinking that
Kennedy was president most of the 1960s or that Gerald Ford was a president during this time frame. Under "want to know," a good teacher can
lead students to include questions about how many presidents were in office from 1960 to 1970 and how long Kennedy was in office. After gen-
erating the first two columns, then students can complete a reading, listen to the teacher presentation, or watch a video of the 1960s to learn
about the time frame. A one-day lesson can be concluded with students

Topic: _____

What I **K**now	What I **W**ant to Know	What I **L**earned

1.

2.

3.

4.

5.

Worksheet 3.2.   KWL Chart

filling in the third column, "what I learned." Surprises in this column might include learning that Kennedy's term of office was relatively short, or that Vietnam actually included parts of the 1950s and 1970s. A KWL chart can be used for an entire unit of study as well.

Flow Charts, Cycle Graphs, and Venn Diagrams

Math and science teachers have been using flow charts for decades, and they have become increasingly useful with computer programming courses. A flow chart can have squares, rectangles, diamonds, and circles, all connected by arrows as decisions in process must be made (see figure 3.2). Flow charts work well for teaching guidelines for solving math problems, as well as teaching steps in a science experiment. They are very effective when a student must make a decision with "ifs" and "thens." Flow charts can promote clear, linear thinking. English teachers may use them for the steps of writing an essay or a major research paper.

Cycle graphs are just a series of circles or rectangles connected in a large circle (see figure 3.3). When teaching anything that repeats itself, this graphic will help students learn which steps cause or flow into others. Again, teachers of writing can use a cycle graph when introducing prewriting, drafts, editing, rewrites, and similar activities. Since so many natural cycles occur in science, theses graphs are very useful to science teachers.

Venn diagrams are used frequently by math teachers to clarify sets of numbers. These graphics work for other fields, too. History teachers can compare and contrast wars by drawing the two circles, then having students list the similarities of the wars in the intersection of the circles (see figure 3.4). English teachers can review two works of literature in the same way.

Outlines

Many high school students still do not have good study skills. Teaching students how to make an outline can be very important. Providing an outline on the screen is an organizer that helps your students as you present new material. In addition, teachers can provide an outline to students with some of the big topics preprinted and then ask students to work together or independently to find the subtopics. After a given

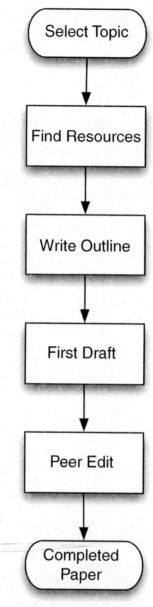

Figure 3.2.   Flow Chart

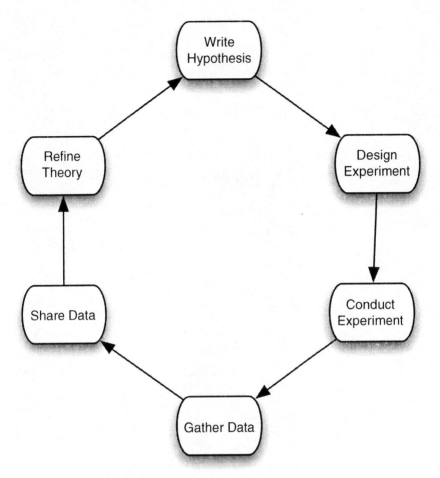

Figure 3.3. Cycle Graph

amount of time, the teacher provides correct answers and more details (see worksheet 3.3).

Using an outline as an organizer is most effective when students interact with the material in a meaningful way, such as having to find answers to fill in the blanks and then doing some speculation as the class discusses the answers. With their organizers completed, students could debate how the course of this battle could have been changed or if a different outcome might have changed the outcome of the war. With the facts of the battle known, students can watch clips of a movie about the war and compare their facts to the movie's presentation of the battle.

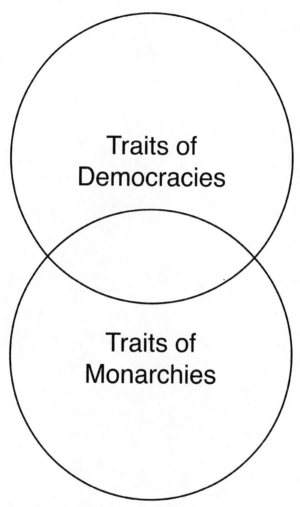

Figure 3.4.   Sample Venn Diagram

Graphic organizers help students to learn facts, enabling them to then think about higher-order issues as a result.

METHOD 4: DEMONSTRATIONS

While a graphic organizer makes a lecture or a concept visual to students, a demonstration takes the presentation into 3D and makes it real. Most students remember demonstrations by their science teachers—and then

The Battle of Gettysburg

I. Events that led up to the battle

   A.

   B.

   C.

II. The Battle

   A. Date

   B. Troops involved

      1. Union resources

         a.

         b.

         c.

      2. Confederate resources

         a.

         b.

         c.

Worksheet 3.3.   Sample Outline

getting to replicate the experiments themselves. Art teachers have often used demonstrations to teach methods of sculpting, painting, and drawing. Music teachers demonstrate special techniques of singing and playing instruments. Physical education teachers demonstrate skills for various sports. What can the rest of us do to present exciting demonstrations?

A history teacher can bring in a suit of armor and demonstrate how cumbersome it was to wear such an outfit. Students can get involved by trying on the mesh shirt of the suit of armor and the visor. The same is true for bringing in a WWII-vintage helmet or gas mask. Some history teachers take students to Civil War reenactments in order for them to see demonstrations of the military equipment and of the utensils for everyday living.

When social studies teachers present information about registering to vote, they can ask a speaker from the county clerk's office to demonstrate how balloting works in the county. Students can each vote electronically and the clerk can tally the votes and see who won the mock election.

What kinds of demonstrations can English teachers do? They can prewrite, write, edit, and rewrite in front of the students on the big screen. They can demonstrate poetry readings and have senior classes do the same for freshman classes. They can use CDs and the Internet to demonstrate lifestyles of the time periods in literature studied. For example, http://65.107.211.206 provides historical information on the Victorian Era, a time period that is often difficult for students to comprehend. The teacher could model clothing of a particular era or have students design a set for a play that they have just read.

Foreign language teachers are models for everything they do. They demonstrate how to speak the language, including how to make nasal sounds in French or how to trill r's in Spanish. They demonstrate the nonverbal gestures that are used by native speakers of the language. They can demonstrate how to cook authentic foods and how to make authentic crafts from the countries studied.

Demonstrations add life to classes. When students get to participate and do their own demonstrations, the learning may be even more memorable to them. Some critics will argue that high school students shouldn't be wasting precious class time by doing arts and crafts or designing a costume that a character in a book might have worn. Proponents of demonstrations and hands-on learning at the high school level argue that these activities will keep students' interest. It has to be better to add some demonstrations than to just start every class for 180 days a year by saying, "Open your books to page x." With the high school graduation rate hovering at only 70% in some states, teachers must make an attempt to make classes active, interesting, and challenging. Clear, direct presentations that engage students' minds can be a factor in raising student interest and achievement.

4

METHODS FOR GUIDING STUDENT TALK AND THOUGHT

METHOD 5: TEACHING WITH QUESTIONS

One way to challenge students and to make them think is by asking tough questions—and waiting for responses that lead to further questions and discussion. When looking at the role of questions in our teaching repertoires, three areas should be addressed:

1. What kinds of questions should be asked?
2. How can we lead students to answer higher-order questions?
3. How should questions be delivered?

Kinds of Questions

Whenever a teacher introduces a new unit, there should be some questions to assess prior interest and knowledge (see worksheet 4.1). Following are some questions I use when I introduce a unit on methods in my college classes. Take a moment to answer for yourself.

1. How did your high school teachers teach their subject?
2. Describe a way that they taught that might be considered a "method."

3. Did you like some methods of teaching better than others? Why?

Questions that assess prior interest and knowledge can occur throughout any lesson or unit, but are a good introductory activity. After all, if a teacher discovers that five students have already read a new novel, that will influence how the novel is taught to the class. Finding out that a student's big brother or sister spent 18 months working in the Middle East could influence that student's answers regarding U.S. involvement there.

Convergent questions. Many questions asked by teachers are convergent ones. Convergent questions have one or more correct answers and lead a discussion to a consensus. For example:

1. What percentage of all teachers are females?
2. Why would more females become teachers than males?
3. What are the major reasons that all teachers give for becoming teachers?

These three questions lead the way for a discussion and presentation of why teaching is often called the most "family friendly" occupation.

Divergent questions. Divergent questions are designed to guide the student to think broadly. There are many possible answers to divergent questions, but answers should be within parameters of what students have read and are learning. A sample of divergent questions that lead teacher education candidates into lengthy debates include:

1. How could our college's teacher education program be improved?
2. How could the student teaching semester be improved?
3. How can the college help you to find your first job?
4. How can the college help you to succeed at your first job?

Focus questions. Focus questions ask students to think about material in a certain way with a given focus. For example, in my orientation to education class, I give the following data: During the school year 2003–2004, the Dekalb County teachers' salaries ranged from $36,900 to $72,828. My focus questions are then:

1. Why is this good news?
2. Why is this bad news?
3. Why are these salaries higher than rural areas to the north of the county?
4. What is the cost of living in this county?
5. What is the cost of a three-bedroom home in this county?
6. Do you want to live there?
7. Do you want to teach there?

Each question is focused on getting students to consider salary versus cost of living for this metro-Atlanta county. Discussion can follow because the types of questions are ones to which students may already know the answers. They can always go online and find some of the answers for further study.

Focus questions are very useful for many subject areas. In social studies, the teacher presents "givens" and directs the questions to the class. In literature classes, the "givens" are from the text and the focus questions are designed to help students understand the plot and character.

Evaluative questions.   Evaluative questions are ones that force students to think, and to perhaps read, research, and debate answers, before forming their own opinion. Evaluative questions are considered higher-order questions as they are not easily answered and require students to think deeply, honing their organizational and logic skills as they do so. Some sample evaluative questions from an education course include:

1. Should the college require courses in English for speaker of other languages (ESOL) for all education majors?
2. Should people with a bachelor's degree in a subject matter be allowed to teach that subject in public schools without certification?

Quick Review of Questions

- Questions assess prior interest and knowledge; find out what students know and are interested in learning.
- Convergent questions ask for one answer.
- Divergent questions generate multiple answers.

- Focus questions make students consider ramifications/consequences after they have been given information.
- Evaluative questions make students dig deeper to form opinions and learn more material.

Higher-Order Questions with Bloom's Taxonomy

While schools stress high scores on standardized tests, they also emphasize the development of students' ability to think. In order to learn how to think, students need to be challenged with questions and tasks that are considered "higher order." Since the 1950s teachers have been learning Bloom's taxonomy as a guideline for teaching thinking skills (see worksheet 4.2). A hierarchical structure, "Bloom's Taxonomy classifies cognitive behaviors into six categories ranging from fairly simple to more complex behaviors" (Orlich et al., 1990, p. 98). The categories of the taxonomy are:

1. Knowledge—a question or task that calls for recall or recognition
2. Comprehension—goes beyond recall and asks for interpretation, translation, examples, or definitions
3. Application—a question at this level involves applying or using information
4. Analysis—involves taking a question apart, looking for reasoning and logic behind the content
5. Synthesis—a question or task that requires students to create a new structure or pattern of understanding
6. Evaluation—questions or tasks that require decision making

Johnson (1990, p. 38) described how an English teacher could ask questions from all levels of the taxonomy when teaching a short story. Her examples are:

1. Knowledge: Where does the story take place?
2. Comprehension: Tell everything about the place where the story happens.
3. Application: Describe a place that you've visited that is like the setting in the story.

Choose a topic in your field: _____

For each of the following question types, list three questions that would help you to begin a discussion, introduce new material, assess student learning, or help students to process and review information.

1. Questions to assess prior interest and knowledge

   a.

   b.

   c.

2. Convergent questions (leading to consensus or one answer)

   a.

   b.

   c.

3. Divergent questions (leading to many answers)

   a.

   b.

   c.

4. Focus questions

   a.

   b.

   c.

5. Evaluative questions

   a.

   b.

   c.

Worksheet 4.1. Five Kinds of Questions for Teaching

4. Analysis: List three ways the setting of this story is similar to and three ways it is different from where you live.
5. Synthesis: Design a poster encouraging people to visit the area where the story takes place.
6. Evaluation: Tell why you would or would not like to live where the story takes place.

Action verbs help teachers to create good questions that reflect the taxonomy. Kellough and Kellough (2003, pp. 156–157) provide examples of action verbs that fit each category of the taxonomy. (Note: the wording and intent of the activity is key to its classification, and not simply the verb selection.)

1. Knowledge: identify, label, list, locate, match, name, recall, recognize, select
2. Comprehension: defend, describe, discuss, explain, generalize, retell, summarize
3. Application: apply, calculate, compute, demonstrate, exhibit, manipulate, plan, predict, relate, show
4. Analysis: analyze, arrange, break down, categorize, compare, contrast, debate, diagram, group, identify, illustrate, infer, organize, outline, relate, separate, subdivide
5. Synthesis: arrange, assemble, classify, combine, compile, compose, constitute, create, design, develop, devise, document, explain, formulate, generate, hypothesize, imagine, invent, revise, rewrite, write
6. Evaluation: appraise, argue, assess, choose, conclude, criticize, decide, estimate, evaluate, interpret, judge, justify, predict, rank, rate, recommend, relate, revise, support, validate

How to Deliver Your Questions

Were you ever in a class where you secretly wished that the teacher would never call on you? How did you avoid being called on to answer a question? Some students volunteer while others avoid the teacher's eyes and questions, sitting sullenly even if called upon to answer. Wait time is an all-important part of delivering your questions. Ask a question, then wait two to nine seconds while students actually compose an

Choose a topic/activity for your field: _____

Now, for each level of the taxonomy, write a question that fits the topic. Your questions will build from lower-order thinking skills (knowledge) to higher-level ones (evaluation).

1. Knowledge

2. Comprehension

3. Application

4. Analysis

5. Synthesis

6. Evaluation

Worksheet 4.2.   Practice with Bloom's Taxonomy

answer in their minds. After your wait time, call on a student by name. If you call on a student before asking the question, only that student has to formulate an answer.

Just as you have to teach all of your routines for classroom management to students, you have to teach students your routines for asking questions. Teach students that there will be times during open discussion when they can simply say or shout out an answer, if that is what you really want, and the other times you will use your "wait-time and call on only one student" system. A teacher who wants to remind students visually of this policy can actually post a stop sign on the front board that says, "stop, wait, think, one answer." When the sign is up, we all follow the policy and when it is not up on the board, a different question answering policy (maybe even shout-out) is in use.

While the wait-time/one-student answer policy can be a good one, some students may never volunteer. So, some days, or parts of some lessons, may need a different questioning policy. Having every student's name on a Popsicle stick and drawing the names out of a cup may be a different strategy to use once or twice a week. It may be a good strategy to use at the beginning of the year until all students understand that they really do have to answer questions in your class. Some teachers keep a small box with everyone's name on a slip of paper for drawing out the name of the student who will answer. They use this box when students quit volunteering. When students are not raising their hands and coming up with thoughtful answers, "the box" appears to jump-start the students a little bit.

Once teachers get students to answer, they have to give feedback to the students' responses. A lot of the teacher feedback is a part of the teacher's overall "withitness" and rapport with students. Some keys to remember about feedback include:

1. If a student answers incorrectly, and another student is allowed to answer correctly, the first student may feel "dumb" and quit volunteering (and thinking). If a student answers incorrectly, and the teacher answers the question, the student should not feel quite as dumb, since the teacher is *supposed* to know the answer and be the expert. A teacher correction is generally better than a student correction of another student.

2. A lot of goodwill is built when the teacher takes a student's attempt at answering and probes or pulls the answer along until the student responds with a truly acceptable answer. Also, wait time is good for allowing a student to self-correct an answer.

3. Students need to know if a response is correct when a question is a factual or convergent one. Therefore, teachers need to respond with yes, correct, right, and other affirming answers. Sometimes a nod or an "ahum" lets the student know that they were right in a very gentle way. Conversely, if an answer is incorrect, students need to know so that they are not learning incorrect information. A simple "no" or "sorry" does not hurt the student's self-esteem but lets the student know that his or her answer this time is incorrect. Again, the best way to proceed is for the teacher to state or explain the correct answer.

4. It is inappropriate to ridicule students' answers at any time. A teacher who makes an insulting response is not acting professionally. Sarcastic responses such as "I guess you didn't study last night because you were out with your girlfriend/boyfriend" or "You may just be too dumb to graduate" are never appropriate. Some teachers say that their use of sarcasm is merited because today's students are "wild and crazy" and using sarcasm makes the teacher accepted by students. However, winning students' attention and gaining their respect does not come from sarcasm. Strong sarcasm is a form of verbal abuse, and teachers are not being paid to insult or abuse students but rather to help them learn and grow.

5. The use of praise in providing feedback to students' answers is also a contested subject. Most argue that praise will raise students' self-esteem and help them to become even stronger individuals. After all, don't we all like hearing that we are good and wonderful? However, when praise is used in providing feedback, care must be taken with regard to the nature of the praise. Praise should be for the answer received, not the inherent goodness of the student. The phrase "Good answer" is fine, as is "You thought hard about that one and solved it correctly." You can even be a little more flowery, if that is your style, "Wow, you figured that answer out with flying colors." What isn't appropriate is "Right as always. You are on your way to being the perfect valedictorian." or

"Just like your brilliant big sister, you are on top of the game, too."
When praised, some students feel extreme pressure to excel even
further, causing themselves stress, ulcers, and genuine sickness.
Praise makes some students feel that they are standing out too
much and won't be liked because of it. Being cool is such a big
deal that some students will work to look dumb just to have more
friends, so praise stops those students from working at all. A general rule may be to simply provide the feedback needed so that
students know a right answer from a wrong answer, and to not use
praise in public in the classroom. Praise may be less controversial
and more effective if used sparingly in private, such as a comment
on a student's paper.

6. Knowing your students and establishing a safe environment in
your classroom is the best way to ensure that students will answer
questions. Remembering how fragile teenagers' egos are and how
strong peer pressure is will help you to not embarrass students as
they strive to learn from your questions.

METHOD 6: DISCUSSIONS

Student teachers often say that their students will not discuss anything.
When I hear this lament, I counter with a series of questions.

1. What was the purpose of the lesson where you tried a discussion?
2. What did you do and what were the students supposed to do (goals
   and objectives)?
3. What is the general level of classroom management like in this
   class?
4. Have the students been taught routines for discussion? Did they
   know what they were supposed to do?
5. How did you plan to use the material from the discussion in the
   rest of the lesson or unit?

In order for a class discussion to work, several conditions must exist.
There must be a reason for the discussion that meets the teacher's goals
and the students' objectives. Students must know how discussions work,

in general, and why they are participating in this one, in particular. Classroom management routines and procedures must already be in place and working in the class. There needs to exist a level of trust among the students and between students and teacher.

What is the difference between asking questions and leading a discussion? With asking questions, the teacher is generally requesting one or two responses from students before asking another question. The communication is teacher-to-student and back to the teacher. With discussions, the teacher is the facilitator, but student-to-student interaction and conversation are expected. Good questions are still the key for good discussions. A discussion may be conducted to lead the whole class to one discovery (convergent) or to lead the group to see that many factors exist behind a problem (divergent). Discussions, just like questions, can get the class to focus or to evaluate.

Discussions that are teacher-led can be used to preview material. For example, asking the class to think about what life may be like in 50 years is a way to introduce a unit on science fiction. Asking students what they would take with them to a desert island may be a way to introduce consumer buying habits and the influence of commercials.

A discussion can be used to help students understand material that they have read outside of class. Questions such as "What did you think of the three chapters that you read for today?" or "Can you relate something in your own life to any of the events in this novel?" can start a discussion of literature that will lead to learning about the plot, characters, author, and background of the piece. Asking students to discuss their thought process when solving last night's math problems not only provides answers to the problems but also lets the teacher know where students may be having trouble with new concepts.

A discussion can review material studied. As students hear other students talking about concepts, the discussion should prompt more questions and a better understanding of the material. The advantage of whole-group discussion is that students are not just being told information but are developing their own learning by hearing other opinions about material. A good discussion can spark students' interest, help them to understand complex material, and allow them to sort the statements of peers by evaluation, a higher-order thinking skill that will always be important to them.

The downside of whole-class discussion is that some students may never participate, or at least not in a meaningful way. Some students, and some teachers and administrators, think that a discussion is also a way out of "really teaching." In order to make a discussion a learning experience, the teacher must let students know why they are having the discussion and what they will do with the material discussed throughout the lesson and unit.

By nature, students are very talkative! Capitalize on their need to communicate by planning a class discussion that has a use within your goals and objectives (see worksheet 4.3).

METHOD 7: GROUP WORK

When whole-group class discussions do not work well for a large class, group work may be the answer for achieving similar goals. Group work became popular when the "cooperative learning" movement swept through K–12 schools and colleges in the 1980s. Before cooperative learning, students had been taught for decades to work independently, to solve problems alone, and often to be highly competitive within the classroom environment. Cooperative group work was based on the premise that in the real world workers are asked to produce a product or make decisions as a group. Businesses reported to educators that graduates were not able to work in groups and therefore needed this type of training in schools.

Robert E. Slavin wrote much about cooperative learning (Kellough & Kellough, 2003; Orlich et al., 1990) and his work indicated that cooperative learning increases cognitive achievement; in other words, cooperative learning increases student learning. Cooperative learning became a very popular teaching method and was validated by many research projects.

True cooperative learning in the form that Slavin discussed it is very highly structured. The teacher forms groups so that students are heterogeneously mixed with regard to gender, ethnicity, learning styles, and academic achievement. Within the group, each student has a role with specific duties to perform, such as materials manager, group facilitator, recorder, reporter, or work monitor. The teacher may preassign the work roles or assign them randomly with numbers or cards.

Topic: _____

This discussion is to (circle one or more that apply) preview material, generate interest, focus students, get students to see one point, get students to see many points, review material, explain material, or other _____ .

Points written on board for students:

1. By the end of this discussion you will be able to ...
2. During the discussion, you will be expected to ...
3. You will use the material/topic/ideas of this discussion as you ... (this relates the discussion to a paper to be written or to a test or an essay)

Teacher questions to start the discussion:

1.

2.

3.

Review of routine for how to conduct a discussion are:

1. Only one person may speak at a time, directing statements at others.
2. Respect all opinions given.
3. Review this routine or post on the board before starting the discussion.

Worksheet 4.3.   Planning for a Meaningful Whole-Class Discussion

Once roles are assigned, students begin working on a given task. The tasks may be problem solving, a review of material previously covered, a discussion of a reading, or a project. Students are given a limited amount of time and specific goals, such as solve a problem and outline how the answer was found by presenting a two-minute report to the class. The accountability of the group work results from the final report to the class, or a paper or project completed jointly. Many teachers who were trained in cooperative learning graded how well the students worked together as well as the finished product.

As cooperative learning became a buzzword in the educational community, complaints surfaced. Students (and their parents) complained that one student would do all the work and all of the students in a group would share the high grade. Some complained that a student could have earned a high grade on the assignment working alone, but that the group's inability to work lowered the grades of the strongest students. Some administrators felt that group work was too time consuming and allowed teachers to work less. Many teachers reported that their administrator would lower their annual evaluations if they observed group work on observation days and not "real" teaching.

Many of the ideas and guidelines of Slavin's cooperative learning, and that of others, have become generalized by teachers in their use of group work. Many teachers use group work very successfully and have never had formal training in any one method of group work. It is now a given that students need to know how to work in groups, but that group work should be one method employed when appropriate, and *not* the only method used by a teacher during a semester. Group work can be an excellent tool for discussions, brainstorming, problem solving, inquiry, review, and role-plays.

What Makes Group Work Successful?

1. Group work is successful when students have a clear set of goals to complete. Students need to know in advance why they are in groups and what is to be accomplished in the group. After groups are formed by the teacher or by choice, hand out a written set of steps or questions for the group. Clarify in the procedures what is to be written by the students at the end of each step or procedure

and how their responses will be shared with the teacher and the class.

2. Time frames must be stated and followed. Students cannot be expected to work long amounts of time without accountability. Setting a timer with a bell makes it much easier to stop groups and have them announce their answers or contribute to the whole class. Having a timer takes the pressure off of a teacher to stop the group work because he or she can say, "The bell rang. I need to hear a great answer from each group." In a 50- to 90-minute class, it helps to divide the group time into 10- to 15-minute units, make groups report to the teacher or whole class, and then go back to their tasks. Allowing longer amounts of time, 30 to 40 minutes before holding students accountable, may result in wasted time.

3. The monitoring of groups is important. In true cooperative learning groups, a student may be assigned the role of group monitor. Some teachers call this role the taskmaster and have students assess other students' participation. Having students assess or grade each other can lead to a myriad of problems, and many teachers find it best to walk around the room and monitor the work themselves. This monitoring time is the perfect time to individualize instruction and to do some informal assessment of students. By being all around the room, teachers can hear students who might not be willing to speak up in a regular class.

4. By being held accountable for a product, an answer, or a presentation, groups will work toward their goal and not just sit and talk about their weekend plans. Holding groups accountable for their work and grading group work overlap. Many teachers give participation points for group work, while others just say that they make students meet class deadlines to come up with answers and presentations that are ungraded.

Group work is often a good way to brainstorm ideas and answer questions from readings. While not graded as a group, individuals who use their time well in the group will hopefully do better on papers and tests that are generated individually after the group work. In order to be fair to all students, grades need to be an evaluation of individual work. For example, students can work together to answer a set of questions from their textbook, or to do an experiment. Grades will be taken from a quiz at a later date that was based on the questions solved by the group, but each individual takes his or her own quiz. A group can do an experiment, but a grade will be given for each student's experiment summary and reflection paper.

Uses of Group Work

Brainstorming.   Have students form small groups (three or four students) to brainstorm ideas for writing a paper, an essay, a poem, or a reflection on a film, a book, or an experiment. After 10 minutes, each student leaves the group and works individually on a title and introduction to his or her work. During the last 10 minutes of class, small groups re-form and each student shares his or her progress with "peer-editing" feedback from the group. Obviously, the teacher must invest in a significant amount of preparation time before setting up this class. Students need to know about how to critique each other in a positive manner and how to edit another's paper constructively, but this can be a very productive class, leaving students with a good start on their assignment.

Problem solving.   Problem solving can take the form of a "think, pair, share" activity, where the teacher presents the problem, allows students to work a set number of minutes individually, then instructs students to pair up and share their solution ideas. After another set time, each pair can volunteer an answer that reflects both of their thoughts.

For groups of three, four, or five, the problem posed must be a longer, tougher, higher-level question. For example, after students read about the Middle East, they can be asked to develop their own "road map to peace" for the region, with each student representing a major faction or country of the area.

Small-group problem solving can be applied to math problems, science experiments, and literature. Asking students to work together to change the plot of a classic novel can be a very creative way to get them to discuss the character and plot as the writer originally developed them.

Role-plays.   Role-playing allows creativity and still gets students to read, research, think, write, and debate. Students can role-play being presidential candidates in a primary election, being heads of government at an economic summit, or being the general who directed a past war. In English class, students can be trial lawyers who put characters on trial for their misdeeds, focusing on what the characters really did and said in a play or novel. The ethics of science can be role-played as well, since having the capabilities to clone or to produce chemical weapons of mass destruction doesn't mean we know how to use those scientific advancements. In a foreign language classroom, students can act as tour guides to a group of visitors, giving a tour of Paris or San José. The presentation of role-plays makes a classroom active and keeps students involved. Students can earn points for participating in their group's role-play, or an assessment can be done later. Students will work hard preparing for their roles if they know that the questions addressed by the role-play are also essay questions on the next unit test.

Review.   Group work can provide a good way to review material. Small groups can work together to write questions that they would put on the unit test if they were the teacher. Next, they can "give" their test to another group, while taking the practice test that group wrote. Of course, the groups then have to grade and return the tests to each other. By assuring students that one question from each group will indeed be on the test, teachers have an instant motivator.

Asking groups to report what they learned and what they liked learning can provide valuable feedback to the teacher as well. Some teachers ask, "If you were to teach topic X to this class, how would you begin?" and "How can I help you to learn this material?" (See worksheet 4.4.)

A Word about Games

Since many teachers use games played in groups or teams, games can be considered a teaching method that stimulates student thought. While games can be a good motivator, there are questions to be considered before using games for variety in your classroom. These questions include:

1. What is the school "climate" with regard to games? Would a principal/parent be concerned about the use of games, insisting that school is serious business in this district?
2. What is the purpose of the game? A game that is used by teams (groups) to review has a valid purpose. A game used to practice skills in math or foreign language also has a purpose.

1. Topic, goal, and objectives
Write out the question/problem(s) to be posed to the groups.
Will you state the problem or do you need to create steps and
give each group specific directions on a card?

Key: Why are we doing this in groups and not as individuals or
as a whole-class?

2. How many in each group? Why?

3. How long for each step of the group work? Why?

4. Accountability: What will the group do at the end of their
work? How will an individual be held accountable? How will
this be graded?

5. What special resources are needed to make this group-work
activity successful? (Props, paper, markers, timer, etc.)

6. Should other teachers, the curriculum director, or principal be
invited in to hear the final reports or watch the presentations?

Worksheet 4.4.   Group Work Planning Guide

3. Is the game being used as a reward, and if so, is this reward meaningful to the students? Ninth graders may find a word game a fun reward, while seniors may not.

4. How competitive is the game? While some competition is good, too much competition can have a negative impact and cause students to withdraw and refuse to play.

Making Games Successful in Your Classroom

Group games tend to be more successful than ones that pit individual students against each other, because peer pressure is rampant in teenagers and no one wants to look dumb. Games that are worthwhile serve as a review of questions and vocabulary from class work. Adopting a popular TV show game can pique student interest and motivate them by letting students "act" the parts of the contestants, the moderator, and the studio audience. Games can be good time-fillers when part of the class has already left for pictures, a pep rally, or sports event, and the students who remain need to be kept busy in a nonpunitive way.

5

METHODS FOR GUIDING STUDENT PRODUCTION OF WORK

In addition to class assignments or homework, students can benefit from working on special projects. Some work should be done in groups, while other work should be done alone, because in the real world, there are times that we work in groups and times that we work alone.

METHOD 8: PROJECTS

We all remember the old science fairs and the projects we created for them. We may also have memories of students whose parents "did theirs for them" and how they won the top honors because of it. The rules for successful group work hold true for successful projects:

1. A clear goal/assignment
2. Time frames that are followed
3. Monitoring of the project—perhaps spending limits or provisions for materials to be provided by teacher
4. Accountability for final project and grade, with clear stipulations about what constitutes "help" from outside of class.

Projects can be done by individuals, by pairs, or by small groups. They generally involve research in a specific area, and an advantage of projects is that students have choices in what they are going to undertake. The wise teacher sets parameters for the choices, perhaps giving a list of 15 authors to the class and allowing groups to research one that they find of most interest. A group activity can stimulate individual projects. For example, groups can research to find the names of well-known 19th-century authors, then each individual can choose an author for his or her project.

The clarity of the goal/assignment will lead to better end products. Tell students in writing what the assignment is and what the finished project should look like. Wormeli (2001) writes, "In the classroom, we can post examples of outstanding projects and papers, discuss the characteristics of excellent work, and encourage students to think about how they can reach the same benchmarks" (p. 60). However, care should be taken in posting work without students' names or grades, and work from previous students should be used instead of current ones, and that work can be kept only with student permission.

Project Ideas

English. Individuals or groups can research an author and the end result can be a presentation to the class about that author. If your school's technology permits, the presentation can be made electronically, on PowerPoint or a similar medium. Be sure to set the parameters of the presentation to include, for example,

- Five facts about the author's personal life (date of birth, place of birth, education, etc.).
- Must include three famous or favorite quotes or short poems by the author.
- Must include one resource that is online.
- The length and type of presentation must be defined.
- If the presentation is a group one, then include an individual assignment for each student that is the majority of the grade, such as requiring each individual to write an analysis of one poem or long quote from the author.

- May include artwork or film clips to bring to class. (Get teacher's approval first, as some films and art may not be appropriate for high school audience.)

History/social studies. Using the same guidelines given for the English project, students can do project work on the lives of famous people who made history. Or students can do projects about their own families or community members, in the style of the *Foxfire* project (Starnes & Carone, 2002). Begun by Eliot Wigginton's work in northeast Georgia (Wigginton, 1985), the *Foxfire* concepts of teaching include having students do original work that interests them and then presenting that work to a real audience beyond the classroom. Students involved with *Foxfire* developed projects that turned into a series of books and a magazine that has been published for over 20 years. The fact that their projects involved interviews with local citizens and the preservation of folk arts made finding an audience outside of the classroom easy, as community members were interested in buying a magazine about themselves. Obviously, not all projects will end with such a success story, and taking student projects out of the school setting requires a large amount of double-checking and monitoring. The results of showcasing students in the community, however, can be very beneficial.

Foreign languages and art. Foreign language study is easily enhanced by projects—for example, map making, cooking, dancing demonstrations, crafts, culture, and the study of famous people of an area. As with any subject, the project needs to enhance and contribute to the learning of the curriculum. When students are learning the vocabulary for food words, they can work in pairs to design a menu that they would offer if they owned a restaurant in a foreign country. This short project can result in role-plays presented in the middle school to motivate students to enroll in foreign language or in a hallway display.

Artwork produced by students in art or foreign language classes can be displayed around the school or in community buildings and businesses. Having a greater audience can be a real motivator and shows the public that something *positive* is happening at the school. Remember that student work can be displayed only with student permission. In this type of display, student names and grade level may be identified. Grades should not appear on any public display of work. If the work displayed is considered a "contest," then students need to know that from the beginning of the project and still need to be allowed to withdraw their work from public display after ratings, awards, or ribbons are displayed, if they so desire.

Other subjects.   Science projects can be very useful, especially if they get students to think and act like real scientists. Students need to cultivate a genuine interest in an idea and then be allowed to pursue their interest a little further. Setting parameters for safety are very important when planning science projects, as well as discussing the safety and ethical aspects of experimentation and research. Projects can be a good way to introduce and develop the concept of original research with students.

Yes, math projects do exist. Project work in math can help students to understand the applications of what they are learning. Using math to figure the cost of a new school building or community center can be a worthwhile project. Show a clip from the movie *Apollo 13* and have students begin a discussion of how math and engineering saved that flight. Then have students design their own projects involving distance.

METHOD 9: LAB WORK

While many adults still remember lab work as dissecting an earthworm or a frog in science class, the widespread use of active learning and manipulatives has broadened the definition and use of lab work. Yes, science classes use labs as much as possible, to replicate experiments and to create original ones. Guidelines for use of labs include:

1. Safety first. Always make sure that every possible precaution necessary is taken. Follow special guidelines for chemicals, fire, and hazardous materials.
2. With the costs of equipment and materials continuing to rise, consider when students can watch a simulation or go to a website for information similar to what they would gain from the experiment. Save the lab for work that will be of most importance for students to see "up close and personal."
3. Labs need constant monitoring. Consider using a student worker from last year's class to help monitor, or delegating a monitor in each area of the lab.

4. Time frames and specific goals must be clearly stated and followed. Put the guidelines on the board or overhead projector, or project them from a computer so that students know exactly which procedure is next.
5. Allow for clean-up *by the students*.
6. An important factor of any experiment is the discussion and reflection afterward. Plan time for debriefing.
7. Hold students accountable by requiring individual reports from their lab work.

Lab work and hands-on learning are no longer reserved for the science class. Every class can take advantage of "labs" creatively. Math classes learn geometry and then go to the gym to measure the height of basketball hoops, or go outside and do some real surveying to practice their new trigonometry skills.

Social studies "labs" can be as simple as the teacher bringing in unique objects and having students speculate on their use, or bringing in old pictures and newspaper ads for student speculation. After the discussion and hypothesis forming, students then use their textbooks and the Internet to test their hypothesis. The links to anthropology and archaeology can be made much clearer as students do this type of work.

With the use of technology, foreign language labs can provide students the opportunity to listen to native speakers while watching them—it is as close to being in the country as virtual reality permits. Teachers not only monitor the students, but labs allow for individual use of the language and provide the teacher with time to work one-on-one with students.

Going to the computer lab—or bringing the laptops to the class—can take the drudgery out of drill-and-practice activities that are still needed in math and foreign language classrooms. A key to using any lab activity is integrating it into the lesson, setting clear goals and objectives, and then assessing student progress made there.

METHOD 10: INDEPENDENT STUDY

According to Kellough and Kellough (2003), "more than ten percent of students learn best alone" (p. 248). As teachers strive to reach *all* learners in today's diverse classrooms, they should remember that teacher presentations and group activities do not work as effectively for all students. In addition, in today's highly competitive era of accountability, the truth is that the work that students do alone (on tests) is generally what gets counted.

When students "learn alone," that process can take many forms: contract learning, self-guided units of study, self-paced chapters, units of study on the computer, or simply having students complete chapters from books and taking tests for mastery. Learning alone can also refer to drill-and-practice activities, memorization, and yes, even worksheets.

Memorization, Drill, and Practice

"Throughout our lives, we need to be able to memorize skillfully. To improve this ability increases our learning power, saves time, and leads to a better storehouse of information" (Joyce & Weil, 1986, p. 91). While much debate has taken place on the topic of memorization and drills as methods of teaching, they still have their place as *one* way of learning. Teachers can help students learn shortcuts to memorizing and enable them to link material memorized to broader concepts. In all fields, there is some knowledge that should be so ingrained that it is recalled automatically, and building the capacity for automatic recall can be a great skill to give students.

Imagine that you are just learning how to conjugate verbs in Spanish. You learn the regular verbs first, and the rules that go with them. Using simple visuals help most students to learn these verbs:

Hablar (to speak)

yo hablo	nosotros hablamos
tú hablas	vosotros habláis
él, ella, usted habla	ellos, ellas, ustedes hablan

When students visualize this format for learning verbs, it helps them as them as they learn other verbs. A similar hint for learning irregular verbs is to remember which ones are "boot" verbs.

Servir (to serve)

yo sirvo   nosotros servimos

tú sirves   vosotros servís

él, ella, usted sirve   ellos, ellas, ustedes sirven

If the student draws a circle around the forms that do not retain the original e of the infinitive, a nice boot can be formed. It is a simple little device for remembering which forms have the e in the first syllable and which ones have the i.

Mnemonic devices were probably used by most students to remember things in elementary school. HOMES reminds us of the lakes that make up the Great Lakes—Huron, Ontario, Michigan, Erie, and Superior. Most professors of education have a mnemonic that they use in teaching the steps of Bloom's taxonomy. My students hum the letters "KCA, ASE" to the tune of the old Mickey Mouse song. They can also remember that King Charles Always Added Sugar Extra to remember that the levels are knowledge, comprehension, application, analysis, synthesis, and evaluation. By teaching our students ridiculous associations, links, or even definitions that they can sing, we are still teaching. It has been well over 30 years since I learned that "a circle is a set of points, riding on a plane, all the points a given distance, from a certain point" and even as I write this, "Jingle Bells" is going through my head. Memorization not only helps our learning power but it also adds to our feeling of success from knowledge. Knowledge is a powerful thing.

It can help to give examples to students to sell them on the fact that there are things that they need to know for themselves. I can multiply in my head, without a calculator. This has been a wonderful skill to possess, as it saves me lots of money at sales. I like sales where things are 40% off of the already reduced half-price. By multiplying in my head, I know the price before I get to the checkout counter. Most checkers don't stop to actually look at an item or figure what the final cost should be; they just scan the item and charge what the computer says to charge. By knowing the price ahead of time, I am sure to get the advertised price.

Independent Study for Mastery Learning

In the late 1960s and early 1970s "independent learning" was a buzz-word in schools. Suddenly, educators became aware that all students didn't learn at the same pace and that self-paced learning could moti-vate some students to go well beyond the minimum standard of the class. I remember a second-year French class that I was in where we worked at our own pace. At the beginning of each chapter of the book, our teacher gave us a contract. The contract specified each activity and quiz to be taken, and when we would be expected to listen to tapes and take oral tests with the teacher. The well-organized teacher had a tremendous filing system; students simply worked all hour at their desks, taking tests and quizzes as needed. She worked with individuals as needed. I loved the system and received credit for two years of French in that one year. Would this system work today? It all depends on the teacher, the students, and perhaps even the level of classroom management in a given class.

Contract learning does not have to be something done all year for every chapter. In fact, it is variety that helps most students to achieve. Consider trying a contract for one unit of study, to be done over a two- to three-week period. If students finish their contract early, they can be given enrichment work, a creative project, or even time to study and write a paper for another class. Many juniors and seniors in high school could benefit from a unit where they paced their learning, earning extra days in the media center to research a paper for another class that didn't allow enough time. Communicating with colleagues can help you choose the right time of the year for this type of project.

Many computer programs may be incorporated into classes and com-pleted by students independently. When a certain program is assigned, all students must have access to the program, and computer availability has to be available to all. In addition, the teacher should do a preassess-ment of skills to make sure that all students are ready for the computer-based study or drills.

Do you remember worksheets from your own school experience? Most of us do. Worksheets are not necessarily bad. A good worksheet can serve for previewing material, reviewing material, or supplementing the textbook. With the right questions, worksheets can address higher-level thinking. As with any assignment, a worksheet needs goals and objectives, and must add to the work being done in class. It should not be a time filler. A good worksheet is a value-added item—and, of course, it must be clear and easy to read.

The down side of independent study and self-guided learning units may be that teachers have to get all students ready for the same tests at the same time. With the accountability movement and its standardized tests, teachers may find that independent study works best on a limited basis. It still has a role in schools, as students need the variety that independence provides, and they need the opportunity to learn how to learn on their own. When they are 27 years old and their washing machine breaks or they have to learn how to find the best mortgage rate to buy a house, they will do so as independent learners.

REVIEW OF 10 TEACHING METHODS

Methods for Teacher Presentations
    1: The lecture/presentation
    2: Concept attainment
    3: Use of graphic organizers
       Webbing, KWL
       Flow charts, cycle graphs, and Venn diagrams
       Outlines
    4: Demonstrations
Methods for Guiding Student Talk and Thought
    5: Teaching with questions
    6: Discussions
    7: Group work
       Brainstorming, problem solving, role-plays, review
Methods for Guiding Student Production of Work
    8: Projects
    9: Lab work
    10: Independent study

6

TECHNOLOGY AND TEACHING

For decades teachers had textbooks and chalkboards and little else at their disposal for teaching. Then media came into classrooms in the form of filmstrips, films, tape recorders, and overhead projectors. The use and overuse of television in schools has been highly controversial during several time periods. As cassettes and videos became prevalent in society, they also acquired educational uses. Computers, DVDs, CDs, Palm Pilots, and every high-tech device on the market can be found in schools now, too. How can teachers take advantage of what is "out there" to improve teaching and to improve the quality of instruction?

TECHNOLOGY AS AN ORGANIZER

Ask any teacher who is old enough to remember typing tests and worksheets on a *typewriter* how technology has improved teachers' lives, and he or she will probably say that simple word processing is the biggest contribution of technology to teaching. It is incredibly easy to update tests, quizzes, syllabi, handouts, and parent letters with simple "cut and paste" strategies. The creation of certificates, cards, passes, seating charts, and other documents is incredibly easy through word processing. The key is to keep your electronic files well organized and easily accessible. The best computer in the world won't read your mind and help you find a quiz that wasn't titled sensibly and filed in the correct folder.

Some of the drudgery work of teaching has been greatly simplified with the computer. Electronic grade books and attendance keepers are a great help to teachers. In fact, attendance and grades are turned in *only* through networked computers in a growing number of schools. As a new teacher, find out what the requirements are for grading and attendance if done electronically, and then get up to speed on that system. If your school doesn't mandate one specific program, just do an online search to find the best program for you. Ask colleagues what they are using. Typing in "grade books" or "electronic grade books" in an Internet search engine will net hundreds of responses.

TECHNOLOGY AS A TEACHER RESOURCE

No matter if your textbook was chosen by you or by the school committee, you will feel that it needs supplementing. Many textbooks come with CDs that provide all kinds of supplemental activities and a myriad of reproducible worksheets, quizzes, and tests. All you have to do is click, print, and copy. Other textbooks come with websites listed at the back of each chapter to help the teacher find more information. Still other texts offer a package for online materials that are updated regularly. Some of these packages include a message board or chatroom where teachers around the country can discuss how they have used the material. Not only can you ask the teacher down the hall for support but now you can also ask any teacher using the text for ideas!

Not even the publisher will include everything that you need. Start a list of favorite sites that are for teachers of your grade and subject area. Again, sites change so quickly that is difficult to ensure that a site listed in this book will still be fully operational when you search for it, but some sites that make good starting places include:

www.teachers.net
www.sitesforteachers.com
www.teach-nology.com
http://rubistar.4teachers.org

When looking at a website, check to see if the "posters" are practicing classroom teachers. Who moderates the site? How often is it updated? Is material given freely according to copyright law?

Some websites have chatrooms that are designed specifically for new teachers. You can also send your questions directly to "experts" at the following two sites, which are sponsored by two national teacher organizations, Kappa Delta Pi and Phi Delta Kappa:

www.kdp.org
www.pdkintl.org

USING TECHNOLOGY FOR VISUALS

I remember going to the school library to find pictures of famous paintings in reference books to show my foreign language classes when we studied artists, and reserving films of the big art museums in Spain and France. Now, teachers can pull up information from the Internet and show the material to students on a big screen. (For example, go to www.louvre.fr/ for the official website of the Louvre and http://museoprado.mcu.es/ for Madrid's Prado. These sites are useful for teachers of art, history, and foreign language.)

English teachers can gain much useful information from websites about authors, both past and present, and some sites provide the living author's e-mail address. Having a picture on the screen of the author as students walk into the room is an automatic attention-grabber and focus activity. Of course, not every classroom will have Internet access and a projector in the room, but many schools have labs and the class can go to the lab for classes where introductions to the topic are given in this format. Even if there is no access in the school, the teacher can use the Internet for the background research and then bring in a few pictures from the search. The possibilities are endless.

RESEARCH ON THE NET

The teacher isn't the only one who can do the research. Students are probably quite adept at researching topics on the Internet. They can research as individuals or as groups. The rules for using the Internet to do research are the same as for any group project: students must have a clear assignment and grading should be done individually, not for the group. The research must fit the objectives of the unit and lesson, and all students must have access to the technology.

In addition to the general rules for doing research or a group project, the Internet may present some unique considerations. Students need to learn that they must sort the information gathered and that just because something appears as a fact on an Internet site doesn't mean it must be true. They need to look for sources of sites. Who created the site and who manages it? Is it a for-profit site? Can they print pictures that appear in the site legally and use them in their report? If students decide to create webpages for a project, then they should work closely with the school's webmaster/site administrator in order to create postings that are usable and that meet the guidelines for the school's website.

What do you do if students are searching for valid information and happen to find totally irrelevant or pornographic material? Well, you are the teacher and you have to monitor the students' use of the computers. If you are online in front of the class, you should know the sites you are going to before class begins, rather than just standing there, typing, and looking. You, too, can be very surprised at what might pop up on-screen. Preview sites just as you would preview any material and make sure that it is appropriate. If you use e-mail pen pals for a class, discuss with the students in advance what can and cannot be discussed. Students may want to invite their pen pal to the United States for a visit and the foreign teenager may accept the invitation and start packing. Discuss the ramifications of the pen pal exchange. In fact, when arranging it with another teacher, outline the rules of writing clearly before ever announcing the project to your students. Obviously, make your administrators aware of these projects and get all the necessary permissions from your district, as well.

COMPUTER DRILLS FOR PRACTICE

The computer may be the best tool invented for skill building. Students can learn how to type with packaged programs, practice math facts, and drill all of the verb conjugations for just about any language with computer work. The advantage for skill building with the computer is that the corrections and feedback are done for the teacher, and the results appear on the screen and can be printed out or put into a grade book, if needed. The computer may hold the attention of some students who would not be thrilled with paper-and-pencil tests. Getting a happy face when a certain number of questions are answered correctly may be a motivator for students. While you can't teach every hour of every day with computer drills, they may be used appropriately with strong results. There are skills that students need to build with practice, and the computer may be just the way for students to build those skills without feeling that the drill is a "kill."

SUBJECT AREA WEBSITES OF INTEREST

Sites can change so quickly that sometimes excellent ones are gone by the time a book is published. The following is just a sample of a few good sites that may help new teachers get started.

Art: (and good sites for teachers of other subjects who want to integrate art into their units)
www.artmovements.co.uk
www.artcyclopedia.com
www.art.com
English:
http://library.thinkquest.org/19539/macbeth.htm
www.ulen.com/shakespeare
www.marktwainhouse.org
French:
www.frenchteachers.org
www.cortland.edu/flteach
History/social studies:
www.gpoaccess.gov
(government documents, plus teacher resources)
www.cia.gov
(world factbook)

www.nationalgeographic.com/geospy
(a great game with states, countries, continents)
www.lizardpoint.com/fun/geoquiz
www.historychannel.com

Mathematics:
www.goldennumber.net
www.gamequarium.com/geometry.html
http://gomath.com
www.mcdougalllittell.com

Sciences:
www.sciencekit.com
www.3bscientific.com
www.cellsalive.com

Spanish:
www.spanish.bz
www.ilovelanguages.com
www.cnnespanol.com
www.spaleon.com
(great practice site for conjugating verbs)

7

HOMEWORK, ASSESSMENT, AND GRADING

HOMEWORK

At the mere mention of "homework," everyone has some memories from past days as a student. There are some people who remember sitting at the dining room or kitchen table and doing homework under the watchful eye of parents while in elementary, middle, and maybe even high school. Others remember sitting in front of the TV and doing homework. Some might report that homework was done in their room with the stereo going full blast while talking on the phone. Many college students say that they didn't do homework in high school, or what limited work they did was done at lunch or in class. Is it really homework if it is done in class anyway?

Homework can be quite controversial. Some parents believe that their child isn't being pushed academically if he or she never has any homework. Others believe that teenagers shouldn't spend so much time on homework that they miss out on teenage fun or working at a part-time job. Many parents don't know what their high school students are doing after school because that time is completely unsupervised for their children.

Another area of controversy is that of who actually does the homework, and whether or not it will be done at all. There are assignments that are meant to be done by students who seek the help of parents or other adults, and others that are designed to be done by a group working together. Some teachers say that since students no longer do homework, they no longer assign it. It sounds as if the homework norms and rules are in gray area, so let's start at the very beginning—with the purpose of homework.

The Purpose of Homework

With a limited number of hours in the school day, the purpose of homework is to reinforce the learning that takes place in the classroom. This reinforcement often takes the form of additional practice in order to make basic steps of learning seem automatic. For example, the math teacher introduces ways to solve problems. Students practice in small groups or as individuals with guidance from the teacher during class and then they can work additional problems on their own to increase their speed and accuracy at solving this type of problem. Speed and accuracy are important for students to attain. I often remember my math homework and how my aunt helped me to learn addition, subtraction, and multiplication so well that there were certain basics I could just do in my head. Those skills served me well on the ACT test, and I still use the math skills that I mastered to a level of automatic. It wouldn't have happened without either the homework or the aunt.

Foreign language is another area where memorizing and drilling certain skills until they become automatic is important. Students who don't master verb conjugation simply can't become communicative in the language as quickly (if ever). Homework can make grammar and vocabulary reinforced to a level that communication in the language becomes a reality. Unfortunately, as a language teacher, I often heard students and their parents say, "I want to speak the language, but I don't want to memorize verbs or vocabulary." For language learning as well as other subjects, just sitting in class watching a teacher and participating in a few activities can't give mastery. Mastery of a subject comes when each individual student learns the material for himself or herself, and that means individual study, which is most commonly homework.

If the first reason to give homework is reinforcement to induce mastery, then the second reason to give homework is enrichment of material that is covered in class. Think about a high school English or social studies class. If students actually read a novel or a chapter about WWII outside of class, then class time can be spent in serious discussion of the piece read. If teachers have to allow class time for all the readings (and many high school teachers are doing this), then the amount of material covered is drastically reduced. We live in an age where students need to know more and more, yet if no readings are done outside of class, then students will actually be exposed to less and less.

Homework can be a way for students to work creatively with the subject matter. I am convinced that I learned to write from the combination of studying writing in class and then going home and *writing* on my own. The same is true for public speaking. In my high school we studied speaking, went home and prepared speeches, then used class time to speak and get feedback for improvement.

Homework can provide a venue for parents, guardians, and extended families to be actively involved in their children's education. Assignments such as interviewing adults about the history that they lived or researching special projects can involve the whole family. When I visited Japan in the 1980s, I was told that a common reason given for an adult not attending a social event was that "he [or she] is helping the children with their homework." Can we dare to imagine a world where families stayed home at least a few nights a week and read and learned *together*?

Having homework can be a good public relations tool for the school. Homework is a visual reminder that learning is taking place at school; when a student brings an artifact of learning home, it is always positive.

To review, homework exists because there simply aren't enough days in the school year for all learning to take place at school. If the teacher is to be a good guide who presents information, engages students in activities, and assesses learning, then it seems a waste of that professional's time to simply watch students read for entire class periods, or to spend hours drilling and practicing basics that might be better learned by the individual outside of class. The case for homework can be a strong one. If homework can be so positive, why aren't all teachers using it and why aren't students doing their homework?

The Case against Homework

First of all, it is unfair to give homework if all students do not have access to the materials and resources needed to complete the homework successfully. In some schools, textbooks are not allowed out of the classroom. If the books can't go home with the students, then they can't be expected to read them or complete exercises from them. Of course, one way around this is to give students a photocopy or handout of the material to be drilled. One of my student teachers recently returned to campus for a visit and told me, "Maybe you should have just taught me how to teach with chalk and a board, since that's about all I have." Having students copy from a board and then go home and solve the problems does still work, but there are newer methods.

Assigning a project that requires construction paper or any special materials can be unfair to those who have no access to materials at home. Needless to say, assigning homework that requires Internet access can't be done unless we can guarantee that all students have access. If they have it at home, great; if not, then provisions need to be made for access in the school's media center or a city library. Again, can all students stay at school or get to the library? If the teacher can't provide the materials and resources when students' families can't, then the homework can't be assigned.

Do students have an environment at home that is conducive to homework? Do they have a desk and lamp? A quiet place to read? Are they at home enough hours after school to do homework? If a junior in high school leaves school for work and then gets home at 9 or 10 p.m., it is doubtful that he or she will do homework. Athletes who are on road trips simply do not have time to study when there is a game. Jobs, taking care of their own children, and all of the extracurriculars available to high school students take time away from studies.

Educators know that they are faced with some fierce competition when it comes to getting students to do academic work outside of class. In fact, educators encounter tough competition when it comes to getting some students to *attend* school, much less work outside of class. Some students have no jobs or family duties and never participate in school-sponsored activities and still do no homework. Others with a myriad of commitments find time to study. A percentage of students at competitive high schools spend so many hours studying and being tutored that their stress levels may be too high. What is the answer?

Making Homework Work

What makes homework effective? The first guideline for homework is to give a meaningful assignment that fulfills an objective. The homework must reinforce or enrich what is being done in the classroom. It should be important and relevant, never just busywork so that there are a few more points to average. The amount of homework assigned has to be achievable. It is insane to expect that ninth graders read *Moby Dick* outside of class in three nights. It is very reasonable to expect juniors and seniors to read several chapters of a novel at night.

There should be open and honest discussion within the school about the amounts of time expected for homework. High schools using some forms of the block schedule have students who take only three academic classes at a time. When students have only three classes, expecting half an hour to one hour per class for outside work can be reasonable. When students have five academics every day, they simply do not have time for five hours of homework every night. The school's mission and culture will reflect how much homework can be expected. College-bound students should be doing homework or college workloads will overwhelm them.

Students have to have the prerequisite background knowledge and skills to do the assigned homework. Class time is a time for the teacher to teach, and for students to practice skills. Homework should be challenging but not overwhelming, and should not be impossible for the student who attended class and paid attention. Resources and materials must be available to all students. In some districts, a teacher cannot presume that students will have magazines or calculators in their home. Of course, in other classrooms, the student body may have many more resources at home than are provided at school.

Every time an assignment is given, the directions must be clear about who is to do the work and how much help can be used. Some students get tutoring after school from professional tutors or college students. As a teacher, you should establish guidelines about which assignments can be done with the tutor and/or parent, and which ones, if any, are to be done without any help. Even when you say that no help can be given, remember that today's students do not necessarily follow an honor code, so saying no help means nothing to some. Since the teacher cannot be in the homes supervising the work, then the teacher cannot grade work lower if it appears that outside help was used. There is simply no way to prove that this is "cheating" anymore. Therefore, teachers give homework and grade it according to other criteria, knowing that some students do their own work and others probably don't. Change the assignment and grading rubric and don't get sued over issues that used to be the norm.

The truth of the matter is that homework is often done assisted, and that is what is commonly accepted. Many teachers tell students that they are encouraged to work in study groups to solve math and science problems, just as they might in a college class or medical school. They are further reminded that the test will be on their own, so that they should each understand how the problems were solved.

When the homework is writing, many teachers encourage students to have a peer read and edit their paper, or even a parent. In the real world, we have colleagues and friends edit our papers before we submit them for publication. Again, if peer and parent edits are permitted, the end product should look better and the grading rubric will have higher quality indicators.

Students should know what will happen to their homework. I have heard of teachers who collect homework and throw it away! Homework is of no use if students do not get corrections and feedback for their work. Another valuable use of homework is to give the teacher feedback on what the students can and cannot do. Some students slide by in class but can produce quality work when given the motivation and time outside of class. Others seem to shine in class with their verbal or interpersonal skills but do not write or problem solve well individually. The teacher needs to know these things before major chapter tests that determine grades.

Feedback, Correction, and Grading of Homework

First of all, students can get feedback and correction of their homework without the teacher assigning a grade to it. Will students do homework if it is not graded by the teacher? Well, the answer is, "it all depends." One technique is for the teacher to spot-check the students' homework for completion as the class begins. If it looks complete, it earns 5 points out of 5 possible. If it looks started and half-done, it's a 3. Nothing means a 0. If a teacher has two spot checks a week, then 90 points of the nine-week grade are homework spot checks and that can be significant. After the spot check, the students can correct their own work as the teacher gives the answers. Students can share answers and the teacher can correct verbally, but students need to see answers as well. Using an overhead projector often works best, as the teacher can put answers on the transparencies before class starts. If the teacher lets students know that some of the exact questions from the homework are on the chapter test, then students have motivation to correct their own papers.

Some teachers may want to collect one assignment a week (or when appropriate) and grade that set of papers. Again, random collections and spot checks should keep motivated students doing their homework. If the assignment is to be graded, students should know how much the assignment is worth and how it will be graded. Rubrics, which are simply designs describing the criteria and quality indicators to be earned for a grade, are very helpful when given when an assignment is made. (Samples appear later in this chapter.) If a formal rubric isn't given, then the teacher should at least explain the grading when the assignment is made. For example, if 20 problems are assigned, each will be worth one point. To earn full credit, the student must show all work and have the right answer.

If homework is graded, then there should be a fair and consistent policy in place for late work. Generally, if a student has an excused absence, the student can turn in an assignment on the day he or she returns to class with no penalty. Students with unexcused absences are generally not allowed by schools to turn in an assignment that was collected while they were skipping the class. Students who arrive in class without homework may be allowed to turn in a paper with a late penalty, but if the answers were given in class, the student can't just copy the answers and expect a grade for that work. Yes, there is some gray area with regard to homework, which is why teachers need to think about the purpose of the homework, how it will be reviewed so that the student gets feedback, and what their policies are before assignments are given.

Lastly, homework should not be given as a punishment. The students' behavior should be corrected with the corrective actions listed on a teacher's management plan; writing sentences and doing more work is not a way to correct student behavior.

Review of Homework

Purposes:

1. Reinforcement of material learned so that students achieve mastery of basics at the automatic level.
2. Enrichment of what is done in class so that more material can be covered.
3. Can give students the opportunity to be creative and go beyond basic learning.
4. Can involve family with student's learning, and can reinforce the value of what is learned in school to the family for positive public relations.

Making homework effective:

1. Homework has to have a valid purpose.
2. Amount of work is achievable in the time frame.
3. Homework, and its length, should fit in the school culture and mission.
4. Students must have the background knowledge/skills.
5. Students must have access to materials/resources.
6. Guidelines must be clear about getting help or working as a group.
7. Teachers must provide feedback and correction for homework.
8. If graded, rubrics should be provided before the assignment is given.
9. Fair and consistent policy for late work should be in place.
10. Homework should not be used as punishment.

ASSESSMENT

One basic definition of assessment is "determining if students have learned the material presented." Teachers need to assess their students because they need to plan how much time to devote to the rest of the topic. Teachers need to know when to move on and when to reteach. Teachers should assess students' learning to know when to give final tests for grades. Students need to know what they have learned and how much more is required. Parents want to know their students' progress. In essence, assessment takes place to inform teachers, students, and parents about student learning. However, parents, teachers, and students are not the only ones who want and need to know the data on student learning. The accountability movement has led the media to report the results of school assessments in every venue from hometown newspapers to CNN. Assessment of student learning takes place at the classroom level and also at the school, district, state, national, and international levels. The question of "how are we doing?" drives assessment.

Key Terms for Assessment

In some areas of education, a difference exists between the words *assessment* and *evaluation*. Assessment is sometimes an umbrella that covers evaluation and other terms, such as grading, testing, and measurement. An assessment is often defined as any way of finding out about student learning. An assessment may be informal and nongraded. An example might be the asking of questions at the midpoint in a 50-minute class. The teacher can tell if more practice is needed or if the class is ready for a new topic. In contrast, an *evaluation* carries with it a determination of some kind about the student learning. This determination generally takes the form of assigning grades, creating a numeric system of ranking of student achievement, or marking a cutoff of pass/fail. However, some textbooks and many school assessment programs use the words *assessment* and *evaluation* interchangeably, with no semantic difference. The best advice to teachers is to use the vocabulary adopted by their district and state, knowing that when they read journal articles or study research, some writers are going to make distinctions and use their own definitions.

Formative assessment means ongoing assessment; while it is often nongraded, it may be graded. Formative assessments are diagnostic, helping both student and teacher know what to do next for improved student learning. An example of a formative assessment that is graded would be an essay in an English class. While graded, the student gets feedback for improvement and the grade for the one essay is not the sole determining factor for a course grade.

Summative assessment is done at the end of a lesson, unit, semester, or course, and is graded. Summative assessment is an evaluation that determines a student's grade and determines if they pass or fail a course. Unfortunate as it may be, the final exam is a summative assessment and rarely gives the student a chance to study mistakes and re-learn material.

The terms *validity* and *reliability* are very important in the discussion of assessment. Validity is "the degree to which a measuring instrument actually measures that which it is intended to measure" (Kellough & Kellough, 1999, p. 419). For example, a valid test about solving math problems measures what is was created to measure—if students can solve the given problems. An invalid "test" of a student's ability to speak French would be an exam where no speaking was required. A valid test of whether or not a student can write an essay is to have the student write an essay. An invalid test of writing an essay would be for a student to complete true/false questions about great essays from history.

Reliability refers to "the accuracy with which a technique consistently measures that which is does measure" (Kellough & Kellough, 1999, p. 420). A simple way to think about reliability is to remember that a reliable test gives the same results if given over and over to the same student. Validity and reliability can be discussed in terms of the tests that teachers themselves take. The standardized teacher exams seem to be highly reliable, that is, an individual teacher's scores do not change much from one sitting to the next retake. However, many teachers argue that a written test does not demonstrate whether or not they can stand up in front of a class and actually teach. Hence, is the test very valid?

Other terms discussed in assessment include *authentic assessment* and *performance assessment*. Tied very closely to validity, these terms refer to a process of assessing a student's ability to do something by actually having him or her do the task, as opposed to taking a paper-and-pencil test about the task. Again, an authentic assessment of writing may take the form of a portfolio of student writing. Performance assessment in foreign language may mean having the student make a tape speaking the language, rather than matching the French vocabulary word to its English equivalent.

Classroom-Level Assessment

Classroom-level assessment informs the teacher and students if students are mastering the objectives for each lesson. Clearly written objectives not only guide the teacher's lesson but also provide the criteria for assessment and testing. Hence, a teacher-made test that assesses the specific criteria to be taught is called a criterion-referenced test. A simplified example follows for a lesson on the Civil War:

> *Objective:* By the end of the *lesson*, students will be able to list events that led to the Civil War.
> *Objective:* By the end of the *unit*, students will be able to discuss the importance of the events that led to the Civil War.
> *Test questions for end-of-unit test:* List and explain the importance of three major events that led to the Civil War.

Throughout the lessons on the Civil War, the teacher should be asking students to list the events, discuss them, write about them, and role-play them. When the time for a summative test arrives, the teacher should know that students are prepared and the students should know that they are prepared.

Some argue that teacher-made tests can be among the most useful assessments, since the teacher knows what was taught and controls the objectives and the test. However, we all remember taking tests in high school where we realized that a test question was asked about something never mentioned in class. How does that happen? Perhaps the teacher used an old test and simply forgot one topic or type of problem, or maybe the teacher used a published set of questions that didn't quite match what was taught. The alignment of what is taught with what is tested is crucial.

Since there can be wide latitude in teacher-made tests, and how they are graded, the standardization of testing has attempted to further quantify if students are learning what they should be. Of course, someone has to define what students should be learning; the writers of widely used standardized tests must use an accepted body of knowledge for each field of study for "what students should know."

District, State, and National Testing

Districts may mandate end-of-course tests to determine if students have actually mastered material before they receive a passing grade for a course, and before qualifying for graduation. The state may mandate such testing as a way to ensure quality of coursework. Depending on the degree of control mandated by the state, the state may use a purchased test from a national company or may have test writers at the state office of education develop one test for all districts. Some states may use committees of teachers to write the tests for the subject areas.

An apparent question becomes, "If the teacher doesn't know what a state-level test covers for a certain subject area, how can he or she prepare students for that test?" Curricular alignment is the answer. Textbook publishers have become so advanced in marketing books that texts are now written for the state-mandated curricular topics, and yes, state-mandated tests. It is certainly hoped that the state-mandated curriculum has been thoroughly aligned with the textbooks used and the test given at the end of a course.

Districts and states use standardized tests to not only assess what students are learning but also to compare students' achievement and to then rank the achievement of classes and schools. Any test that compares the achievement of groups of students is a norm-referenced test. The ACT and SAT are norm-referenced tests at the national level, and the academic achievement of U.S. students is ranked for each state from these and similar tests. There are international rankings of student achievement based on norm-referenced tests as well.

As teachers, it is easy to be overwhelmed by the complexities of all the forms of testing and assessment. The pressure to have students performing well on both criterion-referenced and norm-referenced testing is high. National school reforms, such as the No Child Left Behind Act, are in part based on raising test scores for all students and holding teachers accountable for student learning. At the state level, a state board of education takes action in the cases of low-performing schools, and while "low performing" can be measured by a number of factors, test scores are generally a significant factor. Some districts and states have tried rewarding teachers for high student test scores. The competition can be fierce! Knowing how to write a good test and how to prepare students for a test will help you to cope with the stresses of testing.

While this book is all about simplifying the broadest of concepts for new teachers, you may want to read further on the topic of assessment. See, for example, *Classroom Assessment: Enhancing the Quality of Teacher Decision Making* (Anderson, 2003).

Test Writing

What are the rules for test writing?

1. A teacher-made test should be a criterion-referenced test, testing the objectives covered in the lessons taught.
2. A test should be written well before it is given to the students, not the night before.
3. Students should be tested in the manner in which they were taught and test questions should be indicative of how material was practiced.
4. Students should have enough time to finish the test without anxiety. A timed test is only appropriate if speed is a learning objective. (Example: typing x words per minute)
5. There should be ample room to write responses on the test, and test items should have space between them for ease of reading. More space on a test may actually help to raise test scores!
6. The teacher should write an answer key *before* giving the test and write a reference page back to the textbook or a date that refers to when the material was presented in class in the margins of the answer key.
7. The teacher should predetermine the point values for test items and provide students with that information on the test, as well as provide a rubric for how short-answer and essay questions will be graded.
8. A test should have a variety of types of questions.

Types of Test Questions

Anyone who has completed 12 years of schooling and 4 years of college can probably name the types of questions most commonly found on tests.

- Multiple choice
- True/false questions
- Matching
- Ordering
- Fill in the blank (completion)
- Finish the drawing (completion)
- Short answer
- Essay

Selection Questions

Which types of questions were your favorites as a student? Now that you are the teacher, why will you choose the types of questions that you do? Students will probably say that test questions requiring "selections" were their favorites because these questions provide a chance for a right answer even with a guess. Multiple choice, true/false, matching, and ordering are selection-type questions. Are selection questions necessarily easier? No. Some multiple-choice questions can be very challenging—think about story problems where you had to do long calculations to find the answer before marking which answer was correct.

Basic hints for writing good multiple-choice questions include:

1. Write some introductory material, then a stem, then four responses that match the stem in grammar and in language. Example:
2. For each statement/question, choose the one best answer.
3. The term for when a test measures that which it is intended to measure is
    a. validity
    b. reliability
    c. readability
    d. credibility

4. Vary where the correct answer is placed. There should not be patterns, such as aac, cca, aac, and so forth for the correct answers.
5. Keep responses the same length.
6. Avoid "the use of words such as always, all, never, and none" (Anderson, 2003).

When writing multiple-choice questions, the introductory material should be clear about how many answers are required. Some teachers use multiple choice and tell students to mark all correct answers, knowing that some questions will have one, two, or three right answers. These types of multiple-choice questions can be much harder for students to answer. Before you give your first test to students, you should share some practice questions, and explain if your multiple-choice questions are one-answer only or multiple-answer ones. Is providing practice questions to high school students considered spoon-feeding? No, it is preparing students for the test and it is teaching them how to think and how to take tests. Teaching students how to take tests is another important part of your job as a teacher.

When would true/false questions be appropriate in evaluating student learning? Some teachers find true/false to be appropriate for quick quizzes because they are easy to grade and give a basic idea if students are reading assigned material. For example, an English teacher might give a true/false quiz over assigned book chapters or short stories. The questions are very straightforward—just checking to see if students read the material and know the characters and plot. Be sure to have students write out true and false, or print a capital letter clearly, because sloppy penmanship will cause some Ts to look like Fs. Placing all the blanks at the front of the sentence will make grading easier, too.

For example:

1. _____ True/false questions can be used on quizzes and tests for simple or complex statements.
2. _____ A student has a 50% chance of getting the question right by just guessing.
3. _____ On a multiple-choice test question with four possible answers, a student has a 25% chance of getting the right answer just by guessing, when there is only one right answer.

Matching one item to another is a type of question that can be used. While not necessarily considered good pedagogy, I remember taking many foreign language vocabulary quizzes where we just matched the Spanish word to its English equivalent. These tests were so much easier than ones where the teacher said an English word and we had to write the Spanish equivalent. Current practice in the teaching of foreign language promotes tests where the language is used in more communicative approaches, but I did learn vocabulary using this "laundry list" approach. If matching is used on a test, always make sure that there are extra possible answers on one side of the list, so that students do not get the last one correct out of sheer elimination.

Matching may work better when a student matches names of characters to the appropriate short story, or names of poems to the appropriate author. Again, one has to ask, is the objective of the student learning to be able to identify who wrote what? If so, matching will work. If the objective is to order the events of a war, a story, or the steps of an experiment, then an ordering exercise is appropriate for assessment. The teacher lists many events on the test, and students must arrange them in the correct order. It can be important for students to know what led to what in history; later questions in the test may then ask students higher-order questions about why each event had such importance.

Completion items have drawbacks. Namely, students can guess and earn some points just by guessing. The students do not have to produce the knowledge or facts being tested, they simply have to recognize the right answers. However, there are times when we want students to just recognize the facts. Once they can recognize the facts, then we can go to higher-order learning, which may be tested with production questions.

Production Questions

Fill-in-the-blank (FIB) questions do require students to produce an answer. They must be able to write the missing word or phrase to complete a sentence. FIB questions can be difficult to write and are harder to grade, because there are sometimes multiple answers that are correct. For example:

The _____ is the activity that a teacher prepares
in advance, writes on the board, or shows on a screen to get students started working as they arrive for a class.

Correct answers include sponge, warm-up, hook, opener, and anticipatory set. There may be even more answers. A FIB with only one answer would be

_____ was the 22nd president of the United States.

Grover Cleveland is the only right response. The teacher writing this
question would have had an objective stating that "students will know
the first 25 presidents' names and the order in which they were president." This test question is only valid if students practiced the order of
the presidents' terms and their names. This may not be a good objective,
as there may be more important things to teach in today's history classes,
but the test question is a valid one if it matches an objective and if students practiced the material in class.

A second type of completion item is that of finish the drawing. Teachers of geometry and trigonometry have long used this type of evaluation.
When teaching about architecture, art teachers and history teachers
may ask students to draw types of columns, distinguishing one type from
another. This is a valid assessment if students have been solving problems with drawings in their math classes, or have been drawing columns
in the studies of history and art. It can be very difficult to grade, as the
teacher must make the expectations very clear regarding how much to
include in the drawing for full credit. (More on grading of all work later
in this chapter.)

Students are generally asked to write more often than they are asked to
draw, which means many tests include short-answer and essay questions.
Chapter 4 introduces Bloom's taxonomy for the writing of questions. This
taxonomy can also be used when writing test questions. On the taxonomy,
questions of knowledge and comprehension are at the lower end of the
scale. Application and analysis are in the middle, and synthesis and evaluation are at the top, meaning they represent higher-order questions. It is
certainly important that a test evaluate a student's knowledge—meaning
recall and recognition. Matching and multiple-choice questions test

recognition, the low end of Bloom's taxonomy. Test questions that begin with calculate or compute are application-level questions, and require the students to produce work. If an essay question asks students to argue a point or to evaluate a piece of writing, that is an example of a higher-level question.

To make a valid test, students have to practice exercises in class that are similar to ones on the test. A friend of mine, new to teaching, complained that his students did poorly on tests where he made them synthesize large amounts of material and solve complex problems on the test. "How much practice do you give them in class regarding this synthesis of material and advanced problem solving?" I posed. He replied that he presented in class and the synthesis was the learning part that they had to do on their own. My answer was, "Well, that might have worked in Ivy League schools in the 1950s, or the research-one university where you received your master's, but it won't work in today's high schools." We have to test students the way that we teach them. Yes, we do get to give tough tests with higher-order questions, but that requires asking those same types of questions and forcing the practice of problem solving in class. With high standards of teaching and testing, we can actually get students to do the quality of work that will enable them to attend an Ivy League school or research-one university. Even if they don't go to this type of postsecondary institution, they will indeed need to know how to synthesize information and solve tough problems, because life throws a lot of information and problems at us!

Guidelines for good questions that lead to student production include:

1. Make questions very clear. If you want at least four reasons that America should not have entered a recent war, state that.
2. Include how many points each question is worth, explaining how points are earned.
3. Including a rubric is a good way to have fairness in the grading of the essay question. (Rubrics are provided in the next section of this chapter.)
4. Decide if you will count off points for spelling and grammar. If so, state that before the test, prepare students in how to improve their spelling and grammar, and inform students of the value of spelling and grammar. Will students be allowed to use a dictionary?

5. How will you handle handwriting that is illegible? Will there be students whose special education programs allow them to write the test on a laptop so that handwriting is not an issue? Can other students be allowed to write answers on computers, using spell-checkers and grammar checks? The technology available in classrooms is changing how students take tests.
6. Allow space for writing and provide lined paper, if possible.

Yes, tests where students must produce answers are harder to grade than tests with completion items. They are necessary because students need to be able to write and produce knowledge, not just identify or recognize the right word or term (see worksheet 7.1).

Cheating and Test-Taking Guidelines

Test taking is stressful for our students. Their fears of failing, combined with the pressure to succeed even when they don't have sufficient time to study, lead to cheating. The best way to prevent cheating is to have guidelines for test taking and to adhere to them.

1. Make students put all materials, books, and notebooks under their seats or in their desk.
2. Walk around the room as students take their tests or stand in the back of the room where you can see everyone and they can't see where you are looking without turning around.
3. Tell students that their work must be their own or they will face the consequences of cheating outlined by the school. Tell them every time and write it on the board and put it on a poster in the room.
4. It is sometimes better for you to ask students to raise their hand when done so that you can pick up their test. Student movement in a small classroom can be disturbing to others.
5. You must keep students quiet who are finished—and they must not be allowed to get out their books and check answers while those around them are still taking a test. They can read or study another subject. Having copies of fairly current magazines in the room is a good idea, too.

Choose a broad topic in your field, such as a period of time in history, a genre of literature, or a unit that would be typical in your subject field. For each of the following types of questions, write two examples of test items that would be appropriate for a high school test on this topic.

1. Multiple choice

2. True/false questions

3. Matching

4. Ordering

5. Fill in the blank (completion)

6. Finish the drawing (completion)

7. Short answer

8. Essay

Worksheet 7.1.   Writing Test Questions

6. Do not allow students to get a drink of water or use the restroom during a test. This provides them with an opportunity to go out into the hall, read answers that they have on a piece of paper in their pocket, then return and write those answers on a test.

Before you ever give a test, you need to know your school's policy on cheating. If there is none, then you need to create your own policy and have a mentor teacher or principal read it and approve it. In the past, teachers assumed that students knew rules like, "cheating is an automatic suspension" or "cheating is an automatic zero." This is not the case today. In some schools, cheating means that the test is not counted, and the teacher must create a new one to be administered at a later date. Know the school's policy and then create a situation in your class that prevents the problem from happening.

GRADING

Grading means assigning a value representation to a student's work, and at its best, that grade helps the student and parent know how well the student is achieving. Some people will argue that grading is always subjective, but in order for grades to be fair, grades should be determined in the most objective way possible. For grades to be assigned objectively, each assignment, quiz, or test must have criteria on which the quality of the work will be judged. The criteria should not be a secret! Students should know ahead of time how much each graded piece of work is worth and what they must produce in order to achieve a certain grade.

Grading on the Curve vs. Grading for Mastery

Just what is grading on the curve? The curve referred to in this old phrase is a statistical bell curve, where as many students get an F as get an A, as many get a B as get a D, and the majority of students get the average grade, a C. Grading on the curve is used for sorting students, for making sure that only a small percentage get As and that some fail the course. Grading on the curve is rarely used in high schools today. In fact, it hasn't been used in decades. The most common practice now is for teachers to grade for mastery. This means that a grading scale is established and then applied to all students. Students will not be competing against each other for a grade. All students who make enough points or score highly enough to earn a certain letter grade get that letter grade.

Will grading for mastery cause grade inflation? Well, grade inflation exists because artificial quotas for letter grades are not part of grading for mastery. In some high schools, just like in college, students who anticipate receiving a low grade are permitted to drop a course and repeat it later. Teachers relate that even when grading for mastery is spelled out clearly, some students will choose not to complete the requirements at the quality level needed for a passing grade. With the high school graduation rate in some states hovering at 70 or 75%, we know that many students will not only fail courses but will also fail in their high school program.

Setting Up a Grading Scale

One of the first things that students want to know at the beginning of a new school year is "How will I be graded?" Some teachers have persisted in answering this question by explaining that tests count the most, quizzes count less, and homework will count some, but doing your homework will enable you to have higher quiz and test scores because doing the homework helps you learn the material. Currently, just saying lines like this will not be a sufficient answer for students or their parents. Grading scales for high school classes must be crystal clear from the beginning.

As a new teacher, you will need to find out if your school or department has established guidelines for course grades. One high school had the following system:

Student grades are determined for each nine weeks by the teacher, using the following scale:

93% and higher = A
86% to 92% = B
78% to 85% = C

70% to 77% = D
69% and below = F

Each teacher can determine how many assignments, projects, quizzes, and tests will be graded, and how they will be graded, but each individual assignment should be graded with the 93, 86, 78, 70-percentage scale for consistency with the determination of the nine-week grade.

Once two nine-week grades are earned, they will be averaged. Each nine-week grade is then 1/4 of a semester grade, the average of the two semester grades is 1/4 of the semester grade, and a final exam is the last 1/4 of the semester grade. The final exam must be cumulative, covering all material from the entire semester. In order to average grades, teachers will use a four-point scale for letter grades, with A = 4, B = 3, C = 2, D = 1 and F = 0. No pluses or minuses will be used. For example, if a student earns an A and then a B for the nine-week grades, then earns a B on the final exam, the formula will be: 4 + 3 +3.5 + 3 = 3.375, a B for the semester

The above example is not that uncommon, as schools have been forced to quantify how teachers determine final grades. Some districts have even more complicated systems for the assignment and averaging of semester grades. Many schools use a plus/minus grading system where the distinctions between each letter grade are further delineated. How can a classroom teacher simplify a scale and make it user friendly? A system of total points works wonderfully well for high school classes.

The Simplicity of the Total Point System

A total point system can be applied to percentages set by the district, the school, the department, or the teacher. If the English Department says that all English teachers will use a scale of 92 to 100% = A, 82 to 91% = B, 72 to 81% = C, and 65 is the final cutoff for a D, then total points can be averaged to this scale. If no percentage scale is required by the department and school, then the teacher can set the percentage cutoffs, and the old traditional 90, 80, 70, and 60% cutoffs are fine to use. Why do some schools insist on setting the percentage scale? They feel that a scale slightly above the traditional 90, 80, 70, 60% scale helps them to motivate students and demand higher performance. Why do some departments require all teachers to use the same percentage scale? They are trying to establish standardization of grading, which is almost always controversial in some respect. Imagine being assigned to Ms. Smith's algebra class and learning that you must earn a 94% to get an A, then hearing your best friend say that in his algebra class, an 89% is still an A. Would you want to transfer? Who wouldn't want out of Ms. Smith's class? It is only with objective, criteria-driven grades, applied with consistency, that teachers will not be fending off complaints and lawsuits.

With a total point system, the percentage scale for grades is posted on the wall of the classroom and given to students at the beginning of the semester. Then, students are told how they earn points for everything required in class. Examples:

To earn an A, you must have enough points for a percentage of 90 or above.

To earn a B, the percentage will be 80 to 89%.

To earn a C, the percentage will be 70–79%.

To earn a D, the percentage will be 60–69%.

Earning less than 60% of points will mean an F for the course.

Homework: Homework will be spot-checked for completion randomly. A completed homework earns 5 points, more than half earns 3 points, and half or less earns 0 points. Graded homework assignments vary in point values, but will generally range from 8 to 20 points. To know how your homework grades look, keep track yourself, as follows:

| Your points: | 5 | 3 | 7 | 12 | 9 | 9 | total: 45 |
| Total possible: | 5 | 5 | 10 | 15 | 10 | 12 | total: 57 |

If you have earned 45 out of 57 homework points, your homework grade is then 45/57 or 78%. This is a C. However, note that you are not receiving a letter grade for homework; it is averaged with all the other grades for one letter grade.

Quizzes will be worth 20 to 50 points.

Tests will be worth 50 to 125 points.

Projects will be worth 30 to 50 points.

Essays will be worth 30 to 50 points.

My grade book looks like this:

Your points:	5	17	34	87	3	19	46	12	5	= 228
Total points:	5	20	40	100	5	25	50	15	5	= 265

Earning 228 points out of 265 is 86%. This is a B.

One of the best things about a total point scale is that it lends itself so well to a simple computer grading program or spreadsheet. Even if you don't use a computer to add up the points and then find the percentage, this is very easy to do with a calculator. Many times students and parents will request information about grades before you sit down and compute grades. With this system, you can add up the student's points, divide by the possible number available, and have a percentage that converts to a letter grade. When athletes need the current grades computed for eligibility to play their sport, it is again easy to figure.

Should there be points available for participation? Participation points must be quantifiable if they are awarded. This is *not* a category where a teacher gets to subjectively say, "Well, Raymond didn't bother me at all this nine weeks, so I'll give him 40 participation points out of 50." Teachers cannot grade students on how much they like them or on how little they bothered them! Grades are indicators of academic progress, not behavior, so participation points must be ones earned for going to the board, leading a discussion, contributing to discussions, and so on. Many teachers no longer give participation points because they are too subjective. Remember that parents will complain to administrators about grades in a heartbeat, and yes, you can be sued for capricious grading. Keep your system crystal clear, and award points that are justifiable with assignments, quizzes, tests, and similar evaluations.

In addition, schools have policies regarding student absences. You will probably not be allowed to create your own policy with regard to when or if a student can "make up" work missed when absent. The school will issue excused or unexcused absence lists, and there will be a policy about how students can make up their work for a grade. You can create a policy for accepting late papers. A standard policy is that a student loses 10% per day that a paper is turned in late, with some sort of cut-off date for how late a paper will be accepted. Obviously, spot checks of homework do not have makeups, since the point of the spot check is to determine if students are completing homework in a timely manner.

If participation points are an area of concern, should extra credit points be considered? In my own teaching, students have asked at the end of the semester if they can do extra credit to raise their grade. Extra credit should not be used to allow a student to change a grade at the end of the semester or at the end of a grading period. Awarding extra credit to change a grade at the last minute defeats the purpose of summative grading and certainly takes away from the reliability of grades.

Use extreme caution when awarding extra credit. Extra credit can be used if the points earned are a very small total of the overall number of points to be earned. The points available for extra credit should not total more than 2 to 3% of the total points available. Extra credits must be offered at the same time to all students in the class. Extra credit should definitely involve extra work and higher-order work. Putting one or two additional problems or questions at the end of a test can be a safe use of extra credit points. Letting students know that papers with three additional references will earn extra points is another good way to use extra credit to motivate students to do a little more research. The idea behind extra credit should be motivation to do extra work and learn a little more. Extra credit should not be a way for a student to compensate for lack of studying early in the grading period.

Take the time to complete worksheet 7.2 to create your grading scale. This worksheet should become a page that is shared with students at the beginning of the year and should be included in a newsletter home to parents. Make sure that your scale fits all school-mandated rules and has the approval of your department chair and/or principal. Do this well before you grade the first paper or assignment.

Rubrics for Grading

The integrity of a grading system is based on the clarity and objectivity of how every grade is determined. Rubrics help to clarify how grades are assigned. A simple definition of a rubric is that it is a written scoring guideline for grading. Rubrics have criteria on which the work is graded and quality indicators (see, for example, worksheet 7.3).

Determine the percentage ranges for grades:

A =

B =

C =

D =

F =

Now, list how points are earned and approximate point ranges to be assigned:

Homework:

Quizzes:

Tests:

Other:

Write a paragraph or create a model that explains how students can compute their grade:

Worksheet 7.2.   Your Grading Scale and Explanations of How Points Are Earned

Categories of Criteria	Quality indicators for scoring			
	4	3	2	1
1. Length	10 paragraphs	8–9 paragraphs	6–7 paragraphs	< 6 paragraphs
2. Grammar	0 errors	1 error	2 errors	3+ errors
3. Spelling	0 errors	1 error	2 errors	3+ errors
4. Content	addresses 4 issues clearly	3 issues	2 issues	1 issue

Worksheet 7.3. Rubric for Grading a Short Paper

Each "short paper" is then worth 16 points. This short-paper format may be used over and over for quick assessment of understanding of the readings assigned. Will some students look at the rubric and start writing "cookie cutter" papers that meet the criteria? Yes, they certainly will, but if the teacher creates a more elaborate rubric, then the student will have to create a more elaborate paper to meet the expressed, explicit criteria and the student just may be working and learning more!

Creating a rubric for projects, oral presentations, and research papers is a must. Some criteria might include:

Length of paper or presentation
Quality of content
Correct grammar, spelling
Quality of visuals used with the project or speech
Relationship of project to material
Completed on time

A large project worth 100 points might have 10 criteria and a scoring guideline with 10 categories, which would then total 100 points. The teacher describes quality indicators that would earn the 10, 9, 8, 7, 6, 5, 4, 3, 2, or 1 for each criterion. This is a lot of work for the teacher, but grading then becomes a matter of circling the quality indicator, then quickly adding up the points. The rubric itself is then attached to the project or paper. English teachers do this when grading speeches and presentations and the grading is done when the student finishes talking!

Be careful with too many quality indicators. It may be better to create those categories with point ranges and a description of what true "quality" work will look like for the student (see, for example, worksheet 7.4).

Obviously, long assignments will have more complex rubrics and short assignments will have simple ones. The value of the rubric is to let students know what they have to do to earn the points that will determine their grade. This will hold them accountable for their work, and should motivate them to produce higher quality work.

I. Clarity of voice during speech

Four indicators:

6–8 points   All could hear. Speaker excited the listeners. Showed great enthusiasm. Much change in voice when needed. Used notes effectively.

3–5 points   Moderate enthusiasm shown. Voice changed to motivate listeners part of the time. Referred often to cards, but didn't read them completely.

1–2 points   Little enthusiasm shown. Used yelling or other ineffective voice. Read speech from paper.

0 points   Couldn't be heard. Couldn't complete speech. Laughed/giggled inappropriately.

Worksheet 7.4.   Criteria

Rubrics from the Internet

Teachers do not have to reinvent the wheel when it comes to rubrics, since there are many sources for prewritten rubric templates. As of this writing, some user-friendly sites include:

http://rubistar.4teachers.org
www.teach-nology.com
www.rubrics.com

A quick search on the Net will yield many sites for rubrics. Some are offered by teachers and others by universities. Use what is available and tailor your rubrics to your specific class needs. Create your own template and just fill in the blanks as your assignments change. Can you use the students in the creation of a rubric? Absolutely. Creating the rubric together is a way of teaching the students the material. If you create a rubric together for speeches, you might begin by asking students, "What makes a good speech?" Their answers are the descriptions of the quality indicators and they are learning (and thinking) at the same time. If students themselves state what makes a good speech, how can they argue if they are graded on the quality they agreed upon at the beginning of the lesson? Rubrics can help us clarify and grade fairly, which should also help to lower student complaints about grading (see worksheet 7.5).

Assignment: _____

Total points available: _____

Due date: _____

Criteria:

1.

2.

3.

4.

5.

For each criteria, create quality indicators and a point scale, perhaps on a grid

For 7 points	For 5–6 points	For3–4 points	For 2 points	For 1 point	0 points

Describe what merits the points under each quality indicator

Worksheet 7.5. Rubric Construction

8

CLASSROOM MANAGEMENT AND GETTING THE SCHOOL YEAR STARTED

Some of the biggest myths about classroom management include:

1. There is no way to study classroom management and discipline; you just have to experience the classroom and then learn how to deal with students and their behaviors.
2. Write a good lesson plan and you don't have to worry about student behavior.
3. Do what your teachers did.
4. When all else fails, turn the lights on and off.
5. Don't smile before Christmas.

To combat myth number 1, professional educators have known for decades that good teaching is both a science and an art. The same is true for classroom management: it is a science and an art. The science of classroom management comes from studying the knowledge base—what has been published by those in the field. As theorists, researchers, and practitioners have published their work on management, it has become clear that there is a body of knowledge that can be shared with prospective teachers that will provide them with the skills and dispositions to successfully manage classrooms. Research backs up the claims that those who are trained in classroom management have more effective classrooms (Evertson, Emmer, Clements, & Worsham, 1997).

Myths number 2 and 3 are debunked because today's students are not like those of days gone by; they bring more social and emotional problems to school than ever before. A new teacher may never get to teach a perfect lesson plan if he or she has not first taught and implemented a viable classroom management plan. If new teachers went out and "taught the way they were taught," without the benefit of the knowledge base, they might yell, threaten, and throw erasers, which we know is not the best way to establish management.

Myths 4 and 5 are part of the "folk wisdom" of classroom management. If the art of teaching comes from experience and reflection about what is done, then that explains why many new teachers have been told to observe their cooperating teachers during field experience and to model their ways. Learning by doing has benefits, but a knowledge base of skills will help a new teacher interpret what is observed for validity and reproducibility, and will save him or her from having to experience every possible problem in order to manage a classroom. The folk wisdom of classroom management has been passed down from teacher to teacher, generation to generation (Clement, 2002). Some of it may work and some may not.

Common sense dictates that well-managed, efficient classrooms provide students with a better environment to achieve academic success. Research backs this claim up (Marzano, Marzano, & Pickering, 2003). Talk with any group of teachers or former teachers and you will probably hear that student behavior and classroom management are major concerns and common reasons that teachers cite for leaving the profession. If classroom management is an essential component of student success and teacher longevity, then maybe the debate over the inclusion of management coursework in teacher education programs is finally over and a new debate will center on how to best teach the knowledge base of classroom management.

What does this mean for you as a student teacher or a new teacher? First of all, you need to be aware of a number of writers in the field of management and what kinds of programs they promote. Read as much as you can. For example, the work of Emmer, Evertson, and Worsham (1999) in *Classroom Management for the Secondary Teacher*, Harry and Rosemary Wong's procedures in *The First Days of School* (1998), Lee and Marlene Canter's *Assertive Discipline* (2001), or Richard L. Curwin and Allen N. Mendler's *Discipline with Dignity* (1988). Many websites have more information. Try www.responsiveclassroom.org, www.disciplinehelp.com, or www.positivediscipline.com. Once you begin to read about programs that are currently in use, you will begin to see their many similarities. Many of the authors writing about classroom management cite each other in their work, sometimes critically! You should also read with a critical eye, asking yourself what will work from the program and what will not work. A course in classroom management or reading one book on the subject will not make you an expert, but it will give you a starting place.

In one of the courses that I teach on classroom management, I routinely hand out scenarios that could occur in a classroom. The scenarios range in severity from students who chatter to students who throw desks. I ask my students to then discuss what two different theorists in the field of management would say about this situation, and how they would resolve the situation if it happened to them. On the day that a student throws a desk in your classroom in the real world, you won't have the time to pause, review in your mind what two different theorists would do, and then discuss the situation with three other colleagues. In the real world, a teacher has to make a decision, act very quickly in order to protect the safety of all students in the room, and restore order to the classroom in order to keep teaching. When a situation happens, you will rely on both the science and the art of teaching, pulling an idea from a knowledge base built up in your intellect and supported by your heart. The knowledge base of teaching is wide; so is what we know about effective classroom management. Study the knowledge and apply it.

MANAGEMENT VS. DISCIPLINE

Discipline has a negative connotation and generally refers to a teacher strategy used to punish a student for improper behavior. Discipline may mean the consequence to get a student to change his or her behavior. At its best, discipline means self-discipline, where a student has learned to take responsibility for his or her own actions.

Classroom management has a much wider definition. Management refers to everything that goes on in the classroom and how the teacher manages physical space, students, time, and resources. Failing to plan for management may make the teacher the cause of common classroom problems!

SETTING UP THE CLASSROOM

It has been said that wars are won before the first battle takes place. This holds true for classroom management, since the physical design of the classroom, the temperature, the seating arrangement, and how the teacher starts the first day may mold the management for the entire year. You probably will not be able to change your classroom's location or temperature, but you can design a seating arrangement that works. For starters, get your class rosters as early as possible and determine if there are enough desks for the students assigned to your room. If not, start the request process for desks. If possible, have two extra desks for students who may be added to your classroom. You will also need a desk for yourself, an entrance table, and/or a worktable. The school will probably provide a computer station and an overhead projector with screen.

While desks do not have to be in rows, all students should be facing the front. Try a U shape, or diagonal rows to make the desks fit the space, if you don't want traditional rows. Whatever your design, make sure that you can get to each student's desk, and that all students can see you and the board or screen. Cramped spaces increase the likelihood of minor hitting and bumping instances. Since high school students can be very adult in size, you may need to request some oversized chairs for heavy students. Some students simply cannot fit into desks that have an attached chair; neither can pregnant students.

Your classroom has to be user friendly, with good traffic patterns. Many teachers place a table near the door to the classroom so students can enter the room and pick up materials needed before they sit down. This entrance table can hold an open file box with students' graded papers. When the file box is out on the table, students know to pick up papers from their individual file folder. *This saves time by eliminating the need to ever pass out papers at the start of class.* It also eliminates disruptions caused when a student walks around and distributes papers.

Students should not see others' grades, and having a file folder for each student helps to ensure confidentiality. Students can deposit papers in their own file on the way out the door. A file system for paper collection makes recording grades easier for you, as the folders are always in alphabetical order. You may want a file box for each of the classes that are taught, with a bright label so students know which box is for their class.

What else might be on the entrance table? In some classrooms, books are kept in the room and can be picked up as the students enter. Assignment sheets or worksheets can be out on the table for pickup. Some teachers keep extra paper or pencils on the entrance table. The point of the table is to get students to obtain all the materials that they need for the class in an efficient manner. With large numbers of students, this is especially helpful. Once students have their materials, then they can follow a clear path to their desks.

GETTING TO KNOW THE STUDENTS

It has been said that teachers cannot teach students who they do not know. The corollary to this statement is that teachers can't manage students they do not know. If you don't believe this statement, try being a substitute and you will see how terribly difficult it is to accomplish anything with students who are strangers. (If you are substituting, try some of these activities when you first meet a new high school class. The result of spending even 10 minutes getting to know a class may make the difference between accomplishing something with them and having a chaotic room.)

Seating Charts

You can probably assume that your class rosters are correct. Use the rosters to make seating charts. An efficient seating chart can be made by writing each student's name on a small Post-it note, then attaching each note to a piece of cardboard. Put the cardboard in a clear plastic sheet protector. When you need to move students throughout the semester, and you will, all you have to do is move the Post-it, and there is no need to rewrite the whole chart.

On the very first day of school, hand students a card with their assigned seat (row 2, seat 3, for example, if your rows are numbered). You can also post a seating chart for all to see by writing it on a transparency or projecting it from your computer to the screen. Greet students at the door and then ask them to find their seat. They should also be instructed to read everything that is on the board (or screen), which will include directions for a written in-class assignment.

An advantage of seating charts is that the teacher does not waste time reading names that he or she can't pronounce. The teacher scans the chart and notes any students who did not show up in their assigned seat. After all students are seated, students can then introduce themselves to the class, pronouncing their name for you, and saying one thing about themselves. What should they say? It depends on the grade or subject level. You can ask students to name a favorite book or TV program, a favorite song or movie, or maybe a favorite food. A simple icebreaker may help you get to know the students, and how they answer the question may tell you much about their personality.

What if you start without rosters or with rosters that are only 40% accurate? If the rosters are not accurate, then you need to try a different approach. Hand each student a large index card as he or she enters and instruct the students to read the directions on the board for making a name card. The card should be one that stands on the desk, with their first and last names, and has one interesting fact about them. I often ask my students to draw (rather than write) this fact, just for fun. With the name-card system, students may sit anywhere they want for the first class. When class starts, you ask the students to introduce themselves and to read their interesting fact or explain their drawing. During class, you can use these cards to learn names; at the end of class, collect the cards and you have attendance covered. You may use the cards to make your Post-it seating chart. Most schools require teachers to leave seating charts for their classes on their desk for the substitute teacher.

Many new teachers ask, "Do I have to make a seating chart for advanced or honors classes or even junior and senior classes?" There are many veteran teachers who never make seating charts and who don't do any introductory activities at the start of the first day of class. Some of these teachers don't have to do the get-acquainted activities because they already know their students or because the teacher is a legend and students walk in with respect and self-discipline because of the teacher's reputation. The rest of us need to start with seating charts and introductions. A new teacher can always loosen the restrictions later in the school year, but he or she can never go back to the first day and start all over again. It is much better to start with seating plans and then dispense with them than to start without them and suffer the pain of trying to implement them in November.

Learning students' names will help you become established. In addition, students should know each other's names. You want to create a pleasant work atmosphere in your room, and that can't happen if students do not know each other. Also, high school students can easily become isolated. Too much isolation might result in a student turning into a loner with significant social problems. Students who don't fit into their classes may have higher tendencies to consider violence or other destructive behavior. Use the first few days of school to get to know your students and for them to get to know each other. These activities may help discourage loners and cliques.

Interest Inventories

Just what kinds of things do you need to know about your students? Well, the initial things should be innocuous, just little things that may help you remember who is who. A good way to get to know the students is to have them complete an interest inventory on the very first day of school. The interest inventory can have a few questions about personal favorites (movies, TV programs, music, food, etc.) as well as some questions about your subject matter. Pretests are good to do early the first week of school, and so are learning style inventories, so your first interest inventory can have a few questions about specific previous knowledge needed for success in the class, and how students like to study (see worksheet 8.1).

Assessing Interest in the Subject Matter

It is so easy for students to deny that they have an interest in any topic related to their class work. Yet asking about their interests on paper may reveal that they do have an interest, or at least a little knowledge from a

Name: _____

Year in school: _____

1. My two favorite school or extracurricular activities are . . .

2. My favorite food is . . .

3. The best movie I have ever seen was . . .

4. If I could travel anywhere in the world, I would go to _____
   because . . .

5. On Saturdays I like to . . .

6. I tend to do the best in a class when . . .

7. My goal for this year is to . . .

Subject matter questions complete the survey:

Worksheet 8.1.   Interest Inventory

previous course. The subject matter questions on the interest inventory can be general or very specific. Even the student's handwriting may give you some insights into his or her academic skills.

Here are sample questions for each subject:

History/social studies:
1. If you could have lived in any previous time period, which time would you have chosen and why?
2. Write three lines about an American who changed our country. How did this person make a difference?
3. Write three lines about a person from another country who might be considered a hero. How did this person make a difference?
4. Which U.S. president faced the greatest crisis while in office?

English:
1. If you were a writer, who would be your role model? Why?
2. If you were to write a novel, what would be the title of it? What would be the first line of your novel?
3. Describe your favorite book. Who wrote it and why is it your favorite?
4. Who was Walt Whitman and what was his contribution to literature?

Science:
1. Name a scientist whose work has changed the world. How did this scientist change the world and why do you remember him or her?
2. Chemistry: Who was Marie Curie and what was her contribution to the world of science?
3. Biology: What is the life-form that is most abundant on Earth?
4. What are the basic steps of the scientific method?

Math:
1. Algebra: Solve this problem. Carla must be at work at the mall at 10 a.m. She lives 30 miles from the mall. Assuming the speed limit is 45 in her area, and neglecting traffic, what time must she leave in order to arrive by 10 a.m.?
2. Geometry: Draw a right triangle with a base of 3 inches, a height of 4 inches, and calculate the length of the hypotenuse.

3. General math: Marla intends to buy three sweaters. Each sweater is $19.99. If she spends more than $35 in the store, the store will give her a 15% discount. If the tax rate in her county is 5%, what will her total bill be?

Foreign language:

1. Ask students questions in the target language that they must answer in the language, such as their name, how they feel, and their age.
2. Ask a cultural question, such as "What might you be served for breakfast in a hotel in Spain?"
3. If an exchange student came to our school from Austria, what might he or she comment on as a big difference between the United States and Austria?

Questions about Learning Styles

You may gain some very good information about how students learn best by simply asking them about their study habits and learning styles. You may want to add some of the following questions to your interest inventory.

1. Which of the following is your preferred way to learn—in pairs, alone, small groups, in the whole-class setting?
2. Do you like to see information as the teacher is talking about it, or can you just listen and learn something?
3. Tell me about a time when you excelled in a class. What was different or special about the way the teacher taught that class?
4. Where do you study—at home, at school, or at your job?
5. Does a lot of studying usually mean a high grade for you?
6. As your teacher, what can I do to help you learn this subject this year?

Some teachers may scoff at the idea of asking students for their input, especially on the first day. It is true that some student feedback will not be helpful, as some students will say that nothing helps and they can't learn, or boast that they have never studied and always passed anyway. However, some students will provide meaningful feedback, perhaps telling you that last year's teacher for history helped the most by providing outlines, or that because of their job, they really do need three days' notice for a quiz. If you keep asking students for input, and then talk with them about their responses, perhaps even modifying presentations because of input, students will most probably respond with more meaningful comments as the year continues.

YOUR PERSONAL BACKGROUND TO MANAGEMENT

There are as many approaches to classroom management as there are days in the school year. One approach is to do nothing and hope that all will go well. Another approach is to tell the students that you never liked rules in school and you plan to be their friend, thereby eliminating the need to enforce rules. On the other end of the pendulum is a teacher who decides to rule with the proverbial iron fist and post a regulation for everything. A good starting point for your classroom management plan is to ask yourself what you remember about rules in your high school and to compare your experiences to what you have observed in field experiences (see worksheet 8.2).

While you may have some excellent examples from your own high school experience, remember that schools are continually changing and that what worked for you a few years ago may not work today in your classroom. Good classroom management is complicated and there are no quick fixes or easy answers, but making a plan is a good place to start.

Why have rules and a plan at all? As teachers, we are responsible for our students' safety, welfare, and learning. Rules provide the parameters for creating the safe, effective classroom where learning takes place. Rules protect us, as teachers, from randomly punishing students when they drive us crazy. Rules set the parameters for behavior and teach students responsibility. It is a given that students don't just come into our classrooms, sit down, take out materials, smile, and say, "Please teach me." Even at the high school level, students need to know your expectations for the classroom routines and for their behavior. If a student knows the rules and what happens if he or she breaks a rule, then only that student is responsible for the action.

1. Did your teachers know you as a person?

2. What kinds of rules did your high school teachers use in their classrooms? Did the consequence for breaking a rule seem logical? Did it deter you from breaking that rule?

3. Were there positives or rewards for following the rules?

4. Were rules enforced consistently?

5. Do you remember your teachers getting backup help from the central office (principal or dean of students)?

6. Were there schoolwide consequences/punishments for breaking some rules?

7. What was the worst example of student misbehavior that you remember from your high school experience? Was it violent or did it threaten the safety of you or other students?

8. Do you remember certain teachers who had efficient, well-run classes? Describe their classrooms.

Now, go back and answer each question with examples from your classroom observations or student teaching.

Worksheet 8.2.   Self-Inventory of Previous Classroom Management

CREATING A CLASSROOM MANAGEMENT PLAN

A classroom management plan refers to your plan for rules, consequences, and positives. Different authors use different vocabulary for their plan, with slightly different meanings. Lee and Marlene Canter (2001) use the phrase *corrective actions* for consequences and *positive feedback* for positives. A few years ago teachers said rewards and punishments for the positives and consequences on their plan. One of my student teachers wrote *realities* for the word *consequences*. She explained that when she taught her plan, she emphasized that breaking a rule in the classroom or in life carried a "reality" with it. Choose your wording and be consistent with it.

Before writing your management plan, find out if your new school has a building-wide plan. If so, then the vocabulary and consequences of your plan must mirror that plan. Whenever schools have preset rules about tardiness, fighting, language, and so forth, you need to use those standards in your room. If you don't agree with the rule, join the committee to change it! More and more schools provide a "new teacher institute" where the building's management plan is discussed with all new teachers. One school provides this workshop and then gives new teachers posters and markers to make their classroom plans on the spot before they leave the workshop.

Once you know the school's umbrella policy for management and discipline, you can sit down and decide on three to five rules that you absolutely need to run your classroom. These rules are for *student behavior* only. Your rules with consequences and positives do not address homework, late papers, and so on. For other classroom issues, you can write and teach routines and policies, but your rules are for behavior. Rules for behavior can include:

1. Be in your seat when the bell rings.
2. Keep hands, feet, and objects to yourself.
3. No interrupting, loud noises, or loud discussions.
4. No swearing or put-downs.
5. Follow all directions.

Some teachers believe that all rules should be positive. If you feel this way, then you can rewrite "No interrupting or loud discussions" to be

"Use an appropriate tone and volume of classroom voice." The rule for "No swearing or put-downs" can be rephrased, "Use only respectful language." All of the rules, whether stated negatively or positively, must be enforceable and observable by you. When I was a beginning teacher, my school had a rule for "no gum chewing." I honestly couldn't discern when some students had gum, and quite frankly, I felt stupid trying to enforce such a rule when I had such larger worries. If a student chewed gum and made huge bubbles that burst, then that could be managed by referring to rule number 3 (loud noises). Specific rules are best. The rule of "keep hands, feet, and objects to yourself" is wonderful because it covers so many inane classroom behaviors. It covers throwing a book, as well as hitting, bumping, elbowing, kicking, and so on. It can cover stealing a pencil, too.

THE SUBJECTIVITY OF RULES

While it is admirable to have a goal of "Be kind to each other" or "Be polite in this room," those phrases are not enforceable, observable rules. They are just too vague and subjective to write into your plan. You may certainly encourage, teach, and model politeness and kindness, but don't make them rules.

No matter how you word your rules, you must teach what they mean. Just what is swearing? Does that mean that you won't allow words that are commonly heard on a network television sitcom? Students will argue that if it used on their favorite TV show, then it should be considered socially acceptable. When I was growing up, we couldn't say *crap* in my house without getting in trouble. Quite frankly, *crap* might be a nice acceptable word today—much better than other four-letter words.

Some businesses have implemented rules about swearing. They tend to take the stance that swearing *at* someone is breaking the rule, such as saying "You are a _____." Dropping a heavy box and saying "_____" is not breaking the rule, but is also discouraged. All rules are subjective, and making rules is like drawing a line in the sand. The important aspect of rule making is to remember that we are striving to teach students to behave in a higher standard, so that they will be accepted by society and have more success.

THE CONSEQUENCES

Consequences must be logical. They must also provide students with a "way out" or a way to save face. A consequence is not necessarily a punishment. A consequence should be considered an action taken by the teacher to get the student to correct his or her behavior. Students choose how to behave and therefore choose the consequences and realities of their actions.

One of the best consequences for high school students is a warning. I used to tell my students that when I said, "Get with the program," that was my warning. Telling students to get with the program is a simple, nonconfrontational statement that alerts the student to make a better choice. I have known other teachers who say, "Make a better choice" for their warning line. They teach their students that when this line is said, the student must make a better choice or face a tougher consequence.

Warnings are good because today's students do come to class with stressors in their lives. Imagine being a parent at 16, working 30 hours a week in a dead-end job, and then flunking a history test. We all might want to throw our books in disgust as we sat down to endure another class with those other worries on our minds. Warning students is the way to win them back over to your side—the side of staying in class and doing something productive. When the warning is backed up by a private message of "I need you in my class today, working hard, and I want to come check in with you for a couple of minutes later," it is even more effective.

Consequences that will be posted with your rules will be tiered in their severity. Obviously, a student who comes to class high on drugs and begins throwing desks does not get a warning and a caring private message. Sample consequence hierarchy:

1. Warning—"Make a better choice"
2. The individual conference or the written behavior sheet
3. School discipline referral/school consequences:
   Detention(s)
   In-school suspension

- Parents can be called at any time in the hierarchy
- For severe behavior, the first three steps are skipped and the student goes directly to the school principal/dean of discipline.

When it comes to managing the behavior of 14- to 19-year-olds, just how much can you do? Teachers cannot touch students; they cannot even threaten to touch them. They cannot explode and make idle threats. One high school teacher was walking down an aisle when a student stuck his leg out in a challenging gesture to attempt to trip the teacher. The teacher said, "Move your leg or I'll move it for you." It was an idle threat. We can't kick a student's leg back under his desk. The teacher made such a confrontation that he and the student had a lengthy yelling match and the teacher kicked the student out of class. The busy principal sent the student back to class within 20 minutes and eventually told the teacher to "get control of the room."

Could the high school teacher in this situation have tried a warning? How would the following words have made a difference?

"Scott, make a better choice here. I need to walk to the end of this aisle, and you need to be working on the sentences on the screen. This is your warning and I know you'll get busy." It is hoped that, after a pause, Scott would have moved his leg, and the teacher could have said, "Thank you." The teacher might have had to ignore the rolling of the eyes or a sneer from the student, but the end result would be that Scott is still in class, attempting to learn. Another important point here is that the students always need something to do. Our grandmothers used to say that idle hands are the devil's workshop. There is so much for students to learn, let's keep them engaged and on-task and so busy that they won't have time to consider off-task behavior. It is also important to be prepared with strategies to manage behavior so that we get to teach those engaging lessons.

Individual Conferences and Behavior Sheets

The individual conference used to be the "go to the hall and wait for me" conference. In many high schools today, students simply cannot be sent out into the halls for reasons of liability. You are still responsible for the student's safety and the safety of other students when they are in the hall. In one high school, it was discovered that a group of students were planning the time they would get sent out into the hall for punishment. A student would plan to be in the hall at 11:15, when the hall was most quiet, and a second student from another class would get a hall pass to the bathroom in order to rendezvous with a recently expelled student to buy and sell drugs!

The conference now takes place at the side of the room, or even at the student's desk. If time permits, the student can be held after class for a one-on-one conference. If space permits, the teacher and student should be as far from the group as possible. In this conference, the student sits and the teacher sits facing the student at eye level, explaining why the student's behavior is inappropriate, what should have been done, and what needs to be done now. The teacher should allow the student to have some input in the conversation. These conferences work best when the teacher has a standard format to follow (see worksheet 8.3) and uses a very serious face and voice. The tone of voice is very important because some students are planning to upset the teacher and will consider it a win if they get the teacher to yell or cry. I tell student teachers to actually practice a calm, stern teacher face and voice in the mirror!

One-on-one conference guidelines

1. Tell the student that he or she was warned previously and has now chosen to accept the consequence of a conference.
2. Start the conference by stating which rule was broken and remind the student of what he or she was supposed to be doing at the time of the infraction.
3. Allow for student input, with a positive question. How will you choose to work as you are supposed to? What help do you need from me to work on the task at hand?
4. You may end by asking the student to choose to go back to his or her original seat and work.
5. Record the date and reason for the conference somewhere, perhaps on a note card for the student's file. Some teachers have a form for this conference and fill it out while talking with the student, then mail a copy home to the parent.

If a conference ends with the student behaving and doing something productive—great. If the student erupts in foul language and worsened behavior, call the parent, the counselor, or follow the school guidelines for disruptive students.

The difference between using a one-on-one conference to correct behavior and yelling at a student is that we must constantly try to get students to work and produce and learn. In order to do that, they have to
be on-task and we have to be teaching. Yelling and threatening are not
teaching.

The Behavior Sheet

Sometimes, taking even two minutes out of class to counsel a student
one-on-one takes too much of our valuable teaching time. After all,
maybe the disruptive student craves personal attention and we have just
rewarded him or her! If that is the case, try the behavior sheet. Look at
the sample included in worksheet 8.4 and write a creative one that fits
your school and class atmosphere. One advantage is that the behavior
sheet can be sent home where parents will read it. Documentation is
extremely important to keep if a teacher needs to eventually have a student placed in a behavior disorder or special education setting or alternative education. Some principals require that a teacher attempt to call
a parent and send at least one letter home before implementation of
schoolwide procedures such as detention or in-school suspension. Out-
of-school suspension or a change to alternative school requires massive
documentation, including paperwork that the teacher has tried all possible minor interventions, such as warnings, conferences, and parent
contacts. Find out your school's policies *before* you need to implement
them, so that the documentation will be sufficient to get help for the
student.

SCHOOL CONSEQUENCES

School consequences are what the teacher relies on when warnings,
short conferences, and filling out behavior sheets have not helped the
student to change behaviors. School-supported consequences at the high
school level generally involve detentions and suspensions. Many schools
give the teacher the right to assign detentions directly. The student
serves the detention in the teacher's room after school or in a school detention hall, supervised by someone else. If the teacher supervises the

Student name: _____

Date and time: _____

Reason for conference: Student did not follow rule # _____
More explanation:

What student should have been doing at the time:

How student agreed to change behavior:

What student and teacher can do to prevent future problem:

Teacher signature:

Student signature:

This form will be mailed to parent: _____ Yes _____ No

Worksheet 8.3.   One-on-One Conference Log (completed by teacher)

Student name: _____

Date: _____

List rule broken with a brief explanation:

What I should have been doing at the time:

How I can improve my behavior and prevent this from happening again:

A goal for the next week in this class is . . .

I would like for the teacher to know that . . .

Student signature: _____

Teacher signature: _____

This form will be sent to parents/guardians: _____ Yes _____ No

Worksheet 8.4.   Behavior Worksheet (completed by student)

after- or before-school detention, it is sometimes more of a punishment for the teacher than the student. If you supervise the detention in your own room, make the student work. He or she should do the work that was not completed during the regular class and then some extra. While it doesn't hurt a student to wash desks or clean whiteboards, caution should be taken if asking a student to lift something heavy or do specific work. If a student is hurt while cleaning a classroom in detention, the teacher has liability issues.

Another caution about teacher-supervised detention is that of not having just one student in your room alone with you. A detention in your room should have multiple students or multiple teachers, not just one-on-one. Even with two students and one teacher, leave the door open to the hall and make sure that you have the power to communicate with the central office. If not, keep your cell phone handy. Some schools have eliminated the option of teacher-supervised detention in their rooms for liability reasons and use the schoolwide detention hall instead. Find out what school consequences are available to back up your management plan.

Calling the Parent or Counselor

I once took a group of students to Europe. Two of the young ladies in the group were intent on staying out all night, sneaking in late and tipsy, and then being late to the bus the next day. This behavior started during the very first days of the tour. After conferencing with them, the other chaperone and I sat the young ladies down in the hotel lobby and said, "We are calling your parents. We will explain your behavior and ask them to speak with you about it. After your conversation with your parents, we will then discuss with them your options. You can remain on the trip only if the late nights never happen again. At the next infraction, you are on the plane home. By the way, we are calling collect—at about $3 a minute." The parents were very supportive to say the least, especially when we told them the price of the emergency tickets home during peak tourist season. Sometimes a call to parents or guardians works well.

Calling a parent or guardian works best when you have calmed yourself after the incident, and when you have written out a guideline for what to say. Your guideline notes can fit on a note card and go into the student's file as documentation.

1. Introduce yourself as you wish to be addressed. ("Hello, this is Dr. Clement and I am calling with regard to Patrick Miller, who is in my sophomore literature class.")
2. Verify with whom you are speaking. ("Am I speaking with Patrick's parent or guardian?")
3. State why you are calling. ("I am calling because . . .")
4. State how you have a plan and that Patrick can improve his behavior by . . . or reiterate the behavior expectations.
5. If the parent has input or relevant background on the student and the behavior, listen and make notes.
6. Summarize the parent's input, thank the parent, and remind him or her of positive expectations.
7. Let the parent know how to reach you if needed (school phone and time when you can take a call).
8. Thank the parent and find a way to get off the phone quickly. ("I appreciate the chance to talk and I'm afraid I must get busy and make three other calls now.")

Sometimes there is simply no one at home to take a call. Leave a detailed message in that case. If a parent becomes belligerent or insulting on the phone, hang up immediately and document the call to your principal. If a parent or guardian says that the student is your responsibility from 8 to 3:30, then document that and don't waste your time calling back. As with all strategies, do what work bests for the student and the situation.

Some schools have a counselor who is on-call for teachers. One school has a responsibility center and students may be sent there for quick counseling and "cool-down" time. Some schools have full-time administrators and counselors to back up teachers when students present challenging behavior. Find out who is available and how they can be used.

What if your school has no backup support for you? This should be rare; one result of increased school violence has been better school plans for violence prevention, which starts with support of classroom management and discipline issues (see Canter and Garrison, 1994). However, if there seems to be limited support, begin by talking with some veteran teachers about how they maintain good management in their classes. Rely on your warnings, conferences, and parent support until your school establishes better guidelines.

THE POSITIVES, REWARDS, AND GOOD FEEDBACK

I occasionally put smiley face stickers or gold stars on good papers of my graduate students. I continue to do this because they seem to really like it. As amazing as this sounds, we all need what counselors call "warm fuzzies" from time to time. If my graduate students benefit from a little positive sticker, then teenagers are certainly not too old for some up-beat, positive reinforcement.

This does not mean that we should reward every little good behavior with candy, stickers, or a marble in a jar. The external motivators that have been widely overused in elementary and middle schools seem to have created high school students who are dependent on extrinsic motivators. Please don't blame the elementary teachers—they are just looking for solutions, too, and their token reinforcements stem from how society has changed. The world of today is pretty focused on instant gratification and material rewards. I noticed that a checker at a hardware store had big stars on her nametag. When I congratulated her on the stars she said, "Thanks. Each one means that I did something good for the company. With every 10 stars, I get a $100 bonus in my check." The company is striving to get the desired behavior from its employees with a significant reward system.

Short of giving your high school students $100 bonuses for good behavior, what would they consider a positive for their expected good behavior? What would motivate you if you were a teenager again? Some possibilities include:

Smiles
Positive note home
Positive note to principal (some schools have a principal's nonacademic honor roll)
Free or discounted ticket to school event
Two minutes of talk-time at the end of the hour
Thirty-second early leave from class (if school permits)

Pass to leave study hall for media center/gym

Bring in a favorite CD to play as background music for 10 minutes

It can be hard to set up the positives, since we are striving for internal motivation in our students, yet sometimes a little external reward works. Strive to find a good balance that works for you.

What can't we use as motivators or consequences? Grades and behavior have to remain separate issues. Grades are the evaluation of a student's academic performance, and behavior is not to be tied to academic grades. This issue has been challenged in some schools, but lawyers and lawsuits are going to remain on the side of grades and behaviors as two very separate issues (see worksheet 8.5).

IMPLEMENTING YOUR PLAN

What will make your plan work? The first step is admitting that you need a plan and then designing one that incorporates schoolwide rules yet fits with your philosophy. You need to teach the plan to your students by having it posted in the room, by distributing copies to students and parents, and by discussing it. The toughest part comes next—when students first break a rule, the rule has to be enforced. Every school year has a honeymoon, which may last a few days or a few weeks. If you are the new teacher, the honeymoon may not even last a few days. When the students decide to start testing you, they will certainly do so. Let them know that you do understand management and are willing to enforce the rules. However, also keep them so busy and engaged with learning, that you send the message that the business of school is learning and that you are so dedicated to your students and their education, you *will* enforce rules so that they can learn and succeed.

Elementary and middle-grades teachers spend a lot of time teaching their rules with modeling and role-plays. A little of this goes a long way with high school students! It is generally best not to overdo explanations, but to make the expectations clear and get quickly down to the tasks of the classroom. Students do need to know your routines, and teaching how to turn in papers and even how to write the name and date on papers can be done with modeling. Having all students turn in a paper for

The rules for this classroom are:

1.

2.

3.

4.

5.

The consequences/realities are:

1.

2.

3.

4.

5.

Severe disruption:

The positives are:

1.

2.

3.

4.

5.

Worksheet 8.5. The Classroom Management Plan

2 points of real credit the second day is an example of modeling that works. All they have to do to earn the credit is write the name and date on their paper as you need it done throughout the year. You can teach a routine this way. It would be even better to ask for one answer to an academic question on the paper.

Before homecoming or after fall break, review the rules. After an incident, you may need to have several students stay one minute after class for a reteach of the rules. Don't talk to 17-year-olds like children, and never use the word *children*. Appeal to the fact that they are young adults and use these reteaching moments to further win the students over to your side.

BUILDING CLASSROOM RELATIONSHIPS

For years, the folk wisdom of how to manage a class has included the idea of "winning students over." Winning students over actually refers to building classroom relationships, and a positive student-teacher relationship is a powerful tool in becoming established in the classroom. Building a good working relationship with students involves knowing who they are and meeting their needs (Erwin, 2003). It also involves motivation through dialogue (Kozminsky and Kozminsky, 2003), not motivation with candy and threats. Showing genuine empathy, interest, and concern for students are keys to relationship building. It must be remembered that teachers are not their buddies or pals but the adult teacher who acts in a professional and friendly manner. We talk with students, listen to their stories, and then reinforce to them that while we sympathize, we also need them to move beyond poor behavior. Teachers are supporters and allies of students, and we are also the last line of defense between their success and failure. We have to be tough, enforce rules, and get them to behave and learn, for their sakes as well as our own sanity (see worksheets 8.6 and 8.7).

Before the first day of student attendance:

- ❏ Find out about the school's management plans. What school rules, consequences, and positives do you need to incorporate in your classroom plan?

- ❏ Talk with your mentor or department chair about your proposed management plan.

- ❏ Plan the seating arrangement for your classroom. Count the desks. Secure an entrance table or other furniture.

- ❏ Get your class rosters and make seating charts or have materials for students to make name cards.

- ❏ Make a poster that explains your plan with rules, consequences, and positives.

- ❏ Write a letter to distribute to students and parents/guardians.

On the first day of school:

- ❏ Plan to arrive early and check your mailbox or e-mail for last-minute school announcements.

- ❏ Be at the door to welcome students to your room.

- ❏ Have directions on the board or screen for the seating chart (or hand out directions) and provide directions for what to begin working on.

- ❏ Introduce yourself and have students introduce themselves.

- ❏ Have an interest inventory or short meaningful assignment.

- ❏ Distribute a letter to students about management and one for parents.

- ❏ Begin teaching the management plan.

Worksheet 8.6.   Classroom Management Checklist

Throughout the first weeks:

- ❏ Make positive, get-acquainted phone calls home or send positive e-mails or notes home.

- ❏ Distribute a syllabus about the course content and keep referring to it.

- ❏ Post the directions for starting class with "do-now" or "sponge" activities every day in the same place.

- ❏ Teach your management plan.

- ❏ Teach routines for handing in papers, finding out about missed work, etc.

- ❏ Build positive relationships by continuing to get to know the students. Attend extracurricular activities and parent open house.

- ❏ Reinforce positive student behavior as much as possible. Be positive.

As the school year continues:

- ❏ Reinforce your plan as necessary.

- ❏ Work with colleagues if schoolwide management is nonsupportive.

- ❏ Continue to send communications home via phone, e-mail, or letters.

- ❏ Get student feedback on management and your course.

- ❏ Document student behavior (file of cards or other).

- ❏ Document your own work—including sample letters to parents—in a portfolio for your end-of-year evaluation.

Worksheet 8.6. *(continued)*

For each of the following scenarios, discuss with another new teacher and/or your mentor teacher what you think should be done.

1. During a literature discussion, a student says "I just don't give a fart about what some dead author has to say about life in the 1700s." Does this merit a warning? Is it considered swearing? Would a principal give the teacher a lower evaluation if the teacher does nothing? Practice saying the words you would say to this student in a class of 29 juniors.

2. Immediately after you have given a homework assignment, and 10 minutes to read and start it, a student slams his book shut and puts his head down on his desk. What is your response? Does this break the rule of "follow all directions"?

3. Immediately after you have given an assignment, a student slams his book shut and begins drawing wild designs on scratch paper. What is your response?

4. A football player calls a cheerleader a cow as students are supposed to be working on the warm-up activity on the board. The cheerleader responds that she is not a cow, but that he is certainly a pig. Your response? What is your response if their words are stronger than cow and pig, or are words with more sexual innuendo?

5. While discussing a social studies reading, a male student blurts out to the class, "Phil probably really enjoyed this reading about alternative lifestyles, since he has one. Tell us what it's like, buddy." What is your response?

6. Many teachers report that the behaviors that test their patience aren't really ones where they can point to a posted rule and say, "You are breaking rule 3." Explain this.

7. Share examples of the worst behaviors exhibited by students in your current teaching assignment. What do other teachers say about these behaviors? What have administrators done about these incidents?

8. Discuss the lives of some students who seem to be in continual detentions and suspensions. What can be done to get these students back into the mainstream of a classroom?

Worksheet 8.7. Real-Life Examples

9

DIVERSITY, COMMUNICATION WITH PARENTS AND COMMUNITY, AND PROFESSIONALISM

Diversity, communication, and professionalism are tightly linked for teachers. Teachers who accept the diversity represented by today's students and who get to know their students' parents and communities are professional. Being a teacher means much more than just teaching the curriculum to students. Today's teachers work to help students learn acceptance of each other's cultures and background. Teachers recognize that parents, families, and communities are powerful partners, and that teachers alone cannot give students all the help that they need. More than ever before, teachers need to reach out and network with all the constituencies of a community to offer the best education to students.

Education has long been considered "the great equalizer" for improvement of socioeconomic status. Education is also the vehicle that teaches democracy and "Americanization" of students. There have always been waves of immigration to this country, and today's immigrants come searching for many of the same things that those of decades ago came for—jobs, religious freedom, and a better life. The melting pot or the salad bowl of the American population continues to grow and change, and schools play a vital role in both socialization and the shaping of society.

DIVERSITY AND MULTICULTURALISM

Virtually all colleges of teacher education include a course about the diversity of today's students. Sometimes this course is a part of the introduction to education class or of foundations of education, while other times it is a complete course by itself. Much literature has appeared in the last decade on this topic (see, for example, Bennett, 2003; Davidman & Davidman, 2001; Nieto, 2000; Wardle & Cruz-Janzen, 2004). What are some basics from the fields of study of diversity and multiculturalism that teachers need to know?

Sonia Nieto (2000) writes that teachers approach her over and over with the same concern, "Why do some of their students (usually African American, Latino, or American Indian students and very often poor European American students) fail no matter what they, their teachers, do, whereas other students (usually middle-class European American students and some Asian American students, as well as middle-class students of other ethnic groups) succeed?" (p. 2). She answers the teachers' question with the following:

> Educational failure is too complex and knotty an issue to "fixed" by any single program or approach. To view multicultural education as "the answer" to school failure is simplistic because other important social and educational issues that affect the lives of students would be ignored. . . . However, if it is broadly conceptualized and implemented, multicultural education can have a substantive and positive impact on the education of most students. (Nieto, 2000, p. 2)

Davidman and Davidman (2001) argue that teachers need to be able to teach with a multicultural perspective, that is, to teach about, and for equity of, the many cultural groups represented in today's schools. Bennett (2003) defines multicultural education as "an approach to teaching and learning that is based upon democratic values and beliefs and that affirm cultural pluralism within culturally diverse societies in an interdependent world" (p. 14). What do these definitions mean for teachers?

Acceptance, Tolerance, and Meeting the Needs of Students

After becoming aware of the literature and theories of multicultural education, teachers need to ask themselves the following:

How do I make sure that all of my students feel accepted?
How do I work to make my classroom a place of tolerance for all?
How do I meet the diverse needs of my students?

While attending a conference several years ago, I heard a young kindergarten teacher tell other new teachers, "I am tired of working so hard to teach children whose own mothers are on welfare, sitting around watching TV and doing nothing. After all, I am working and paying their income. It just isn't fair. I'm willing to work hard to teach, but the children's parents should be working, too. I'm just their babysitter, so that they have even more free time." Another conversation that I heard in a teachers' meeting is similar. A high school teacher said, "That child lives in the trailer court. She skips school all the time and then I am supposed to be here after school to tutor her. That's a waste of my time and effort. We all know that child won't go anywhere or be anything."

As teachers, we must accept all students who walk through the classroom door. This is part of the definition of "public" schooling. If we choose to teach in a private school, we must accept all students because they have chosen and paid to attend the school because of its mission. Acceptance means recognizing that diversity exists, providing opportunities to all, and helping students accept each other with tolerance. The diversity that exists includes differences in socioeconomic status, racial background, cultural background, religion, language, gender preference, and the issue of legal immigrant status. Teacher education programs work to train teachers to overcome their own personal biases and to accept each student who comes into their classrooms as a "whole" student, who is a unique and special package. We accept all students, their parents, their guardians, and their communities and provide all students with the same high-quality education.

How can teachers get to know the community where the school is located? When most job candidates prepare for their interview, they go online and read about the school's demographics. The school report cards that districts prepare are generally available online and contain demographic information. Numbers such as "free and reduced lunch" can serve as indicators of socioeconomic levels in the school community.

During orientation, many schools take new teachers on a bus tour of the community or do a walking tour. Schools are used for events that are open to the parents and community, such as sports events, fairs, and meetings of organizations. Attending these events will help you to become acquainted with members of the community. Your presence at community events demonstrates your willingness to get to know the community and neighborhood served by your school. Acceptance is a two-way street—as you work to get to know the community, you are also working to be accepted by the population served in the community.

Commitment to Raising the Achievement of All Students

After acceptance of who the students are, teachers need to work on the tough part of diversity—raising the achievement of all students to a high standard. I have often heard my own student teachers return to campus and say, "If they just spoke English, I could teach them, but how can I teach ninth-grade biology to students who don't even know basic English vocabulary words?" I have also heard, "I can't assign homework because my students are working almost full-time and they won't do homework. How do I teach all of the material in 11th-grade English if my students won't read outside of class?" Actually, these are tough questions, for any educator. The *academic* diversity of the student body of a high school is probably the single biggest diversity issue that exists. If 10th graders are reading at a second-grade level, it will certainly affect how the class is taught.

Again, teacher education programs and staff development provided by the school districts are aimed at providing teachers with the tools to teach diverse student bodies. Some of these tools include training in ESOL (English for speakers of other languages), courses in Spanish or another language spoken by a significant number of the student body, training in the teaching of reading, and courses in how to adapt coursework for students with exceptionalities (special education and gifted education). It is important that teachers realize that they cannot be expected to know everything before they begin their teaching careers, and that the school district should provide help and specialized training for teachers.

Teachers should not work in a vacuum when it comes to meeting the needs of all of their students. Teaching can be a very isolated job, with teachers working in individual rooms day after day. However, virtually all schools have special education teachers, specialists in ESOL, counselors, translators, school nurses, and other support staff. Teachers have to reach out to these other specialists and work with them. Some schools are called "full-service" schools, as they provide breakfast, lunch, after-school programs, family counseling, day care for the children of students, immunization programs, orientation for recent immigrant students and their families, and other services. Take advantage of the services provided by the school to get help for your students.

Districts have many names for their "diverse" and "low-achieving" schools. One district calls their lowest-achieving schools "high-priority" schools. These schools tend to have the highest populations of low socioeconomic students and non–English-speaking students. The district rewards teachers for staying in high-priority schools with annual bonuses and extra travel and staff development monies. It makes sense to call these schools "high-priority" ones, as raising the standards for all students should be a high priority for teachers and administrators.

Acceptance of students for who they are and where they come from does not mean that we accept their low achievement or accept their fate in life as a done deal. The kind of acceptance discussed in this chapter refers to accepting with tolerance and welcoming arms. We accept students where they are academically, socially, and linguistically, and then we challenge the students to learn and grow and achieve to the highest potential. We are not and should not be accepting of labels, of old clichés about students, and the fact that others may have already given up on these students. The students who challenge us and our old ideas the most may also be the students who need us the most.

Teaching Tolerance

How are diversity and tolerance issues integrated into our academic curriculum? Some schools have character education programs with a curriculum that includes the teaching of diversity and tolerance as required topics. These topics may be taught during homeroom, school assemblies with guest speakers, or integrated into all classes. Most schools observe Black History Month, Martin Luther King's birthday, and Cinco de Mayo with special events to raise student awareness.

The teaching of literature has always lent itself to the study of tolerance, since so much literature deals with human suffering. Of course, it is how the teacher deals with the literary themes that makes the literature a true catalyst for student discussion. Most of us probably read *The Diary of Anne Frank* in high school. My own English teacher made the Holocaust come alive for students. She also compared Anne Frank's date of birth to the birth dates of our parents. When I realized that Anne Frank was approximately the same age at the time as my own mother, who was alive and relatively young, her death seemed even more cruel and untimely to me. My mother kept old letters that she wrote in the 1940s and, of course, she had always kept a diary. Suddenly, that lightbulb of awareness went on over my head. I think that I would have been deeply touched by the story of Anne Frank whenever I had read it, but by having a teacher who shared her own stories of being a teenager in World War II, and her teaching technique of comparing Anne Frank to our own parents, truly made the reading of the work memorable. Memorable lessons provide deeper reflection and learning for the student.

History and social studies classes lend themselves to discussions of the intolerance of people with each other. Many history texts include the imprisonment of the Japanese Americans during WWII as a significant topic for study. The civil rights movement is another major topic studied in history classes. Since so much history involves war and violence, these classes can be an excellent venue for discussions of peace and tolerance.

Theater departments in high schools may choose to present plays that stimulate discussions of diversity and tolerance. Will such plays be controversial? Perhaps they will, but the controversy around a play can also be a teachable moment for the students involved in the play and for those attending. Teachers who teach controversial material must build a climate of acceptance for the material to be taught before their teaching begins. This climate includes discussing the material with the principal and perhaps the board before the unit is taught or the play goes into rehearsals.

Textbooks themselves can lend credence to the study of tolerance and diversity. While most textbooks are now considered "multicultural" in tone, some have a wider variety of diverse topics than others. When you get to choose a textbook by serving on a committee, look for texts with a wide breadth of topics for discussion of multicultural issues. Textbook publishers began incorporating pictures representing diversity many years ago, but pictures alone are not enough. I ask my teacher education students to do an assignment where they review new textbooks in their fields, looking for diversity. The pictures generally rate high on the students' scales, and every year students report that they have found "the required picture of a person in a wheelchair." As you choose texts, go beyond the pictures and look at the deep topics. It is hoped that, as teachers do this, they will also get their students to go beyond the superficial and see the big picture.

COMMUNICATION WITH PARENTS AND FAMILIES

Practical Points of Communication with Parents and Families

If there were rules for communicating with parents and families, those rules might be:

1. Communicate early.
2. Make the first communication positive.
3. Communicate often.
4. Remember that not all students have parents, but every student should have a caregiver.
5. Don't overwhelm families with educational jargon.
6. Be inclusive by inviting families to events/conferences.
7. Remember that parenting a teenager is a challenging endeavor.
8. Remember that this student is someone's pride and joy, making some communications emotional.
9. Be aware that using the word *parents* may alienate some students who don't have parents and some caregivers, so try to use the word *family* or other inclusive term. Some argue that "parents or guardians" may be used, while others feel that guardian may sound too formal. Discuss the wording used in your school with a mentor or veteran teacher.

Written Communication

If at all possible, find out who your students will be before the first day of school and send an introductory letter home to the student and family. If this is impossible, then the letter can be sent out early in the school year. Letters that are mailed home probably have a higher success rate of arrival than letters sent home with students. As with all written communication sent to students' homes, the letter must be typed, easy to read, and no longer than two pages. The letter must look and sound absolutely professional. What should this introductory letter contain?

1. A short paragraph about you, your credentials, and interest in teaching at this school.
2. A short paragraph about the subject, its importance, and why you like teaching it.
3. A list of some of the big topics and how this material will help the student with preparation for the high school graduation test or SAT/ACT.
4. An invitation to meet the teacher at the first open house, with time and place indicated.
5. Information that lets parents know how they can reach you, preferably with the school phone number and the time when you can take a call. E-mail is another great option.

Many teachers are using e-mail for correspondence to families and create a website for their classes. While this use of technology is wonderful, it only works when the community is one where the vast majority (if not all) of parents use e-mail. If e-mail is used, be sure that paper copies are sent to families without e-mail, and that those families have equivalent options for finding out about homework assignments and other information that is "posted." (See worksheet 9.1 for an example.)

Later Written Communication

I have heard it said that many parents choose private schools for their children because private schools tend to have better communication with families. All schools can have good communication throughout the school year. After the initial letter goes out, there should be a follow-up letter about grading and classroom management policies early in the first semester. Teachers should send home the

Dear Families,

I am delighted to begin a new school year at Jefferson High School and look forward to working with your student in Spanish class. I certainly remember being in high school and taking my first Spanish class, which opened so many doors to the world for me. I was able to study in Barcelona, Spain, when I was in college earning my degree with teacher certification, and I spent last summer in Mexico.

While Jefferson High School's Spanish program is based on exceeding the state's curriculum goals for Spanish, we also include some great activities, such as our annual paella cook-off and the dance-around-the-world dinner. Recent research suggests that students who study a foreign language may score higher on their SAT and ACT tests, so your student will not only be learning how to understand and speak Spanish, but the grammar learned may help with English and test-taking skills.

I would like to take this opportunity to invite you to Jefferson's first open house, which will be held on September 19th, from 3:30 to 8 p.m. Teachers will be in their classrooms from 3:30 until 7 to meet with parents individually, then there will be coffee and refreshments in the cafeteria from 7 until 8 p.m.

Please know that I can be reached at Jefferson High School from 2:15 until 2:55 during school days. The number is 777-123-4567. My e-mail is mteacher@xyz.com and I am happy to answer questions you have regarding the school and the Spanish program. I will be sending out newsletters with "hot topics" and exam dates every nine weeks. Please go over the letter with your student and talk with him or her about the class. I anticipate a very good school year. Thanks for your help and support.

Worksheet 9.1. Sample Introductory Letter

equivalent of a syllabus every three or four weeks, outlining topics and exam dates. If both students and a family member sign the syllabus, then that is a great help for holding students accountable for their learning. Yes, creating a syllabus for a high school class takes planning and work, but planning ahead is very important. If a syllabus goes home, then students can't answer the question "What did you do at school today?" by saying, "Nothing." Teachers have to be public relations experts when dealing with their constituents, and those constituents include the parents, families, and caregivers of students. Some members of the public really do believe that teachers do not work hard enough and a syllabus might just help to change that image. In some schools, all correspondence sent to families must first be given to the principal for reading. Even if the principal doesn't want to preread your correspondence, be sure to provide a copy for him or her for the files and always keep a copy for yourself.

In addition to newsletters or sample syllabi that are sent to all families, there will be occasions when personalized, individual letters are sent to parents. A copy of a personal letter must also be kept in your files. These files can be used in a court of law, so remember to write professionally! If your computer hard drive is your "file," then that can be subpoenaed, as well.

Individual letters that are sent home should not always be about problems. Elementary teachers are great about sending home "good news notes" and high school teachers should follow that example. In fact, make a "good news note" template (see worksheet 9.2) and use it frequently. The template can be printed and you can add a few handwritten lines about how the student earned an A on a tough test, or improved in class participation.

When a parent/family member needs to know about a concern, then that letter should be written in a clear, straightforward manner. Having a template may help, as well (see worksheet 9.3). Even when the news going home is negative, attempt to find a positive, such as, "While this test grade is very low, there are enough grades left in the nine weeks that your student can still receive a passing grade (C- or higher) for the course." Some guidelines include:

Make a statement regarding your concern for student.
State the concern/misbehavior/low academic achievement.
State the results of student's action or lack of progress.
State how student can improve, stay in the class, etc.
Make a statement about your support or the school's support.
Remind parents of your contact information.

Date: _____

This is just a quick note to inform you that your student,
_____, has done something noteworthy.
Let me tell you about your student's success:

Sincerely,

* * * * * * *

Good News Today

Date: _____

I have the following good news to report to you about
_____:

Sincerely,

Worksheet 9.2. Good News Note

Dear _____, (Using family member's name is best, if known)

I am writing to inform you that _____ has not turned in any homework for the last six assignments. Since each of these grades is now a zero, your student is at risk of failing the class.

Homework is important because it provides the practice needed to master the subject. Questions on all quizzes are homework problems, and the unit tests will mirror the work done on homework.

I suggest that your student attend the Wednesday afternoon study sessions held in the cafeteria from 3:15 until 4 until he [she] learns to complete homework without the assistance of the Wednesday sessions. While our school cannot "require" this study session, it is a positive way to get students to do their work.

It is early in the semester and many more grades will be averaged into the final grade. At this point, your student can still earn enough points to receive a passing grade for the semester. I am supportive of your student's efforts and hope that we will see a turnaround in the homework. If I can answer any further questions, please do not hesitate to call me at Jefferson High School, phone 777-123-4567 between 2:15 and 2:55. You may also send a note to the school or e-mail me at mteacher@xyz.com. Thank you for your support and I look forward to seeing _____ in class on Monday.

Sincerely,

Worksheet 9.3.   Other Sample Note

Should Letters Be Translated?

If you are fluent in a language spoken by the students and families, by all means translate your letters. Some schools may provide an ESOL teacher or a translator who can provide this service. However, be extremely cautious about using a computer program to translate a letter. These programs translate word for word and may miss the meaning entirely.

Calling Parents

Believe it or not, teachers dread calling parents as much as parents dread getting those phone calls. A new teacher once told me that when she had to call parents, she silently wished that they wouldn't answer. However, a call to a parent can be a powerful tool in communicating with families.

When should you call families? Pretend that you are a parent or guardian and that your own student committed the behavior or received the grade in question. Would you want to know about it? Would you want a phone call about it? Here are some scenarios to consider. Would you want a phone call from your child's teacher if he or she . . .

- Failed to turn in more than four homework assignments in a row?
- Failed a major chapter test?
- Received school sanctions for cheating?
- Skipped class?
- Skipped more than one class?
- Was released from a sports team?
- Was the victim of harassment or foul language?
- Was a top student on end-of-course tests?
- Won a lead role in a school play?
- Had the mumps?

As these scenarios indicate, there can be calls home for positives and for negatives. In fact, if every teacher made a positive phone call home at the beginning of the school year, then later follow-up calls wouldn't be quite so difficult for the teacher or the family member. Applying the test of "Would I want to know if I were the parent?" remains a good litmus test for whether or not to call.

Once you have decided to call a parent, there are some guidelines to follow. Above all else, never make a phone call when you are still angry with the student or upset about the situation. Take time to cool off before calling. Write out what you plan to say on a note card or on a worksheet template for calls home, and then make your call. You may certainly leave messages on voice mail or answering machines. Know that messages are not always heard by the intended recipient, however; teenagers may arrive home and erase messages.

Likewise, parents may call you. Many parents refuse to believe that teachers have limited time at school for phone calls and think that you should leave your classroom in order to take their calls. Your school district should be supportive of your limited time for phone calls and of your need for an unpublished phone number at home. However, when messages are received, every attempt should be made to return calls in a timely manner.

There are times when families are simply resistant to calls from the school. If a family member indicates that he or she is too busy to help you or that the student is your responsibility from 8 a.m. until 3 p.m., then document that response and don't call again. If it is apparent that a language barrier exists, thank the family member and then end the call, noting that you couldn't complete the conversation in your documentation.

Sometimes the best way to end a phone call is with an invitation for the parent to follow up with a conference. Schedule that conference and then end the call. (See worksheet 9.4 for a checklist.)

The Parent Conference

Just as with written communication and phone calls, it is hoped that the first contact with students' families is a positive and/or social one, such as an open house at the school. Once you have met families in a nonconfrontational setting, follow-up conferences are much easier to handle. Of course, some parents will initiate a "conference" when they see you at a basketball game or at the mall or in a restaurant. It is always best to limit how much you say in public, without documentation to back up your statements. Tell the parents that you would be happy to meet with them at an appropriate time to discuss specific issues. You may have to be rather assertive about this. The challenge is always to be diplomatic and assertive at the same time.

Scheduled conferences with family members should be conducted in a very businesslike manner. When the family member arrives in your

Check each as you do it for a reminder:

❏ Today's date _____
   Time: _____
❏ Introduce yourself immediately.
❏ Verify with whom you are speaking.

1. I am calling because _____
   _____
   _____
   _____

2. State what the student can do about this problem/concern/
   academic issue.
   _____
   _____
   _____

3. State how the parent can help the student with this concern/
   issue.
   You can help by _____
   _____
   _____
   _____

4. If the parent provides comments/feedback, record it.
   _____
   _____
   _____

5. State a positive _____
   _____
   _____
   _____

6. Find a way to get off of the phone by saying _____
   _____
   _____
   _____

Keep this worksheet in the student's file for documentation.

Worksheet 9.4.   Worksheet for Calling a Student's Home

room for a conference, always stand and shake hands. This is a must. No executive working in a big corporation would ever miss the initial welcome greeting and handshake. Your job is as important as that of any business executive and it is up to you to show the public that teaching is a profession. After the greeting, take care of introductions so that you know how to address those at the conference and they know how to address you. Introduce yourself as you want to be addressed; some teachers choose to be addressed by their first names and others not. The region of the country may affect how teachers are addressed by their students' families. Finally, provide adult-sized chairs for adults. If at all possible, talk with the adult(s) at the conference by sitting side-by-side with them at a table, rather than staying behind your desk and forcing them into a student desk.

What do you do if the parents bring other adults, younger children, or their child to the conference? When scheduling conferences, let parents know if the conference is just for the adult family members or if it is to be a conference with the student present. If a translator comes with parents, include him or her directly. If a family member who has some guardianship arrives with the parent, they should definitely be treated as an integral part of the conference. In actuality, getting a father, stepmother, and mother and stepfather at one conference can have advantages—and challenges! The advantage is that all involved with the student would get the same story. However, some parents have custody agreements that forbid the other parent from even receiving grades about the child, so find out who is responsible and deal only with the court-assigned parental guardian. If someone drove the parents to the conference but is just a neighbor or other uninvolved party, offer him or her a chair and a magazine in the back of the room or the hallway, but make it clear that you need to conduct the conference with the student's immediate parents/guardians. If small children arrive, offer them a desk with paper and crayons at the back of the room. Some schools provide a coffee break room and child care during afternoon and evening sessions that are devoted to parent conferences.

Who should support you at the conference? Most conferences can be conducted just by the teacher, but if you have any concerns about being in your room with the parent(s), you may always involve another teacher or a school counselor or administrator. When scheduling the conference, let the parents know who will be there and why. Some unions provide a clause that the teacher's union representative may be at any conference, and do not hesitate to use this person if it helps you to conduct the conference. If you begin a conference alone and a parent or family member becomes belligerent, insulting, or appears intoxicated, end the conference immediately or get backup help from the office. Some school districts hold parent conference nights in the gymnasium or cafeteria, with parents waiting at a coffee area and then going to a teacher's table at a set time. The advantage with this setting is that teachers are not isolated, and both teachers and family members must keep their voices in a relatively low, professional tone, since others are just steps away.

Once the logistics of a conference are organized, then you can concentrate on planning what you will say. Since a picture is worth a thousand words, having a student's file is a good starting place. If a parent arrives and it upset that her child received a D for the semester, then sitting down with her and showing her four chapter tests, with grades of C, D, D, and F, will give her a clear picture of how that grade was determined. Showing a parent copies of syllabi also reinforce that you have done your job of informing students and parents of work required. (I had this conference several years ago. As soon as the mother saw her son's handwriting on the tests, she said, "I can't read his writing." When I responded that I couldn't either, and that he rushed through tests, she and I began to discuss how we could get her son into a counseling group and that he would have to start working on some very basic skills.)

Just as with parent letters and phone calls, have an order for your conferences. State concerns, then possible solutions, and get parent support for one or more solutions. Listen to parent input, but don't let parents blame the child's past teachers and experiences. You can express sympathy for the past, but redirect the conference to the present issue. Limit the time for conferences by explaining that others are waiting or that you have a class to teach. You may also end a conference by scheduling another conference for a follow-up. Always thank the parents and put your corporate business skills to use by standing, shaking hands, and walking the adults to the door.

Conferencing with parents can be a powerful tool for improving student performance. Remember to talk about the student in terms of performance and behavior. Strive to state facts, such as "Megan does not turn in assignments regularly," as opposed to "Megan is careless and lazy about homework this year." Remain businesslike, assertive, and very diplomatic. Reassure families that you want their student to achieve success.

Conference Reminders

1. Find out who schedules conferences, if they are held on one day or a series of evenings, and how they are scheduled. For these events, dress professionally.
2. If you schedule individual conferences, find a time that is convenient and determine if you need another teacher or administrator present.
3. Have some documentation ready to present at the conference.
4. Provide adult-sized chairs and a table for the conference.
5. Use handshakes and greetings to open the conference and a handshake and positive comment to end it.
6. Set your agenda and be aware of time.
7. If you and the parents work out a plan, you must follow through with it.
8. Document the conference and keep the documentation in the student's file. You may want to provide the principal or counselor with a copy.

PROFESSIONALISM

Building Bridges with Colleagues and Administrators

True professional teachers not only build bridges with communities and families but also with their colleagues and administrators. Being a new teacher is like being a new employee in any field because you have to prove yourself to your colleagues and you have to find your own path to fitting in and being accepted. When new teachers are hired, the veteran staff wants them to achieve success, because weak teachers may actually mean more work for others. Start out with the attitude that the teachers in your building want you to succeed, and that most will help you if you ask diplomatically.

Some new teachers find that the veteran staff is negative, cynical, and counting the days until retirement. You may have already heard not to go into the teacher's lounge because you will be eaten alive there. As a new teacher, I vividly remember a veteran teacher saying to me, "You seem half-smart. Why did you become a teacher and why are working *here*?" If you meet cynicism and negativity in some colleagues, you can avoid them, assertively defend yourself, or kill them with kindness. There are a lot of unhappy people in the world and some of them will be your colleagues, wherever you work.

Realistically, what can you do to put your best foot forward and become accepted at your school? Doing your job in the very best possible manner is one way to gain acceptance. Learn other teachers' names and greet them whenever you see them. Ask about their day, their weekend, or their family. Don't listen to gossip or repeat it. Sometimes you can simply say, "I'm new, so I can't get involved in this" if a negative situation is evolving.

Attend meetings on time and listen attentively. Do your own homework before making statements that will show your lack of knowledge. A new teacher was in a faculty meeting where the school's test scores were announced. She said, "How could any responsible teachers let this happen? What were all of you doing the last four years?" This is not a way to make friends. The teacher simply did not understand how hard it was to get that school's student body to attend class, much less score well on end-of-course standardized tests.

Work diligently in your room, but get out of your room and make some friends and acquaintances. If the teacher's lounge is a negative place, find the place where the positive teachers gather or create a place where a few teachers can eat lunch or take a coffee break together. Many principals report that they hire positive new teachers in an attempt to raise the level of morale in their school. You may be a change agent, but don't try to change the world in a day.

Attend some sports events and compliment the coaches on what they do. Attend the plays and thank the teachers who sponsored them. Get to know your teacher association representatives and attend those meetings as well, so that you know firsthand what is going on and so that you can have a voice in decision making.

If you are assigned a mentor, learn what that mentor can and cannot do for you. Do not expect your mentor to photocopy tests at the last minute for you, but do meet with him or her when time is available and bring your questions to the meeting so that something can be accomplished. Remember that your colleagues are also as busy and stressed as you are, so their time is valuable.

Remember that secretaries and custodians are your colleagues, too, as well as the cooks, bus drivers, nurses, and psychologists. Learn their names and speak to them. They can be your lifesavers. You would not want to work in the old one-room schoolhouse environment where the teacher also had to mop the floor and cook soup for the students, would you? Appreciate the people who assist and support your work and make it easier.

New teachers who work hard sometimes report that other teachers tease them for their diligence and work ethic, saying that "You will learn to do less" or "You will burn out soon enough." Every teacher has to find a way to deal with these comments. One new teacher said, "I'm doing what I was taught to do and I'll continue helping my students this way, but thanks for the comment." She then smiled and walked away—assertive but diplomatic!

Another way to build bridges with colleagues is to keep other teachers informed. Some schools use a huge whiteboard in the teacher's workroom for announcing field trips, games, major events, and even test dates. If your school doesn't have a schoolwide calendar for this, suggest one. Put your own classes' dates on the schoolwide calendar well in advance, and respect other teachers who have announced dates this way. You must read your mail, whether on paper or e-mail, and stay informed about what is going on in your school.

Think for a moment about your own high school experience. As a student, were you aware of any teachers who did not get along with each other or who disagreed in front of students? Did you ever hear that a teacher was "in trouble" with the principal? Students should not be aware of the internal politics of the school, but most of us can remember such squabbles when we were students. Teachers who "tattle" or gossip about their colleagues should realize that students will find out and that makes everyone look unprofessional.

The best advice for getting established at your school may be to be honest and to be yourself. Be professional, keep yourself updated, and treat others the way you would want them to treat you. If a concern arises, seek help from a mentor or trusted friend. Don't try to change the world overnight, but change the world through your positive actions. Be willing to learn and always keep the students' best interests in mind. If you had a role model from your own days in high school, emulate him or her. It may not be easy to form the kinds of bonds with your new colleagues that you had with your friends from college, but positive bonds will eventually grow.

Working for and with Your Administrators

What does the administrator really expect and want from new hires? The principal wants you to succeed as much as you do, since a successful new teacher makes the principal's job much easier! The principal expects that you will be at school, on time, and prepared to work. All administrators want their teachers to dress like teachers and to act professionally when out in public. If you want to go out for pizza and beer, that's fine, but don't go to the students' favorite pizza place, and make sure that if students do see you drinking, that they don't see you drunk or driving. Proper conduct inside the classroom and outside of the school are both vitally important.

With the nuts and bolts of behavior out of the way, the next thing that the administration wants is for you to keep students engaged and on-task, hopefully with meaningful work that meets the state's curriculum standards. Classroom management and instruction are very important for all teachers, and new teachers must meet the minimum expectations for controlling classes and getting students to learn. Your students' attendance and test scores may be used to determine your effectiveness as a teacher, so motivating students to be in class and to learn while there is a big part of your job.

Principals expect that you keep your room organized with posters and bulletin boards, and with the desks in rows or groups. Yes, even *your* desk should be relatively neat, since you are being judged almost every day as a new teacher.

You will be evaluated by visits from your principal and/or other administrators. Some evaluations are announced and others are not. You can always be proactive when it comes to observations by actually inviting your administrator in to see a lesson or activity that you are especially excited about. While the invited visit may not be "countable" for district evaluation guidelines, it should help to open communication with the administrator. Just the act of inviting a principal into your room will be considered an act of good faith on your part and should help in building a working relationship with the administrator.

Principals do not like surprises, so keep your principal in the loop by providing copies of all correspondence sent to students' homes, especially letters to families and syllabi. If any topic or activity that you plan for a class could be construed as controversial, discuss it with the administration ahead of time. Principals do want to help, as much as their time and duties permit, so build a relationship where you can talk with your principal about a question or concern. Some principals do not get involved with the day-to-day issues of the teachers, and will simply refer you to the department head or your mentor if you have a specific question. Part of learning how to communicate with your administrators is learning who to turn to with different questions. Find a mentor or ask a teacher across the hall until you "learn the ropes."

Don't forget to compliment the boss when he or she wins an award or has a notable accomplishment. When administrators need help, help out if you can. The best relationship that can be built between teachers and administrators is one of collegiality. After all, it takes the commitment of everyone in the school to make the school work.

Role-plays for Communicating with Families and Administrators

To practice for a parent conference or a meeting with a principal, discuss the following with another teacher, actually saying what you would say in the meeting. When you do need to do an actual conference, practice or discuss what you might say with a colleague also.

1. Janine Scott has called the office to talk with you about a student, Carl Fine. You do not know the relationship between Janine and Carl, but the secretary informs you that Ms. Scott will arrive at 1:10, at the beginning of your preparation period. What do you do

at the beginning of the conference? What do you do if you check Carl Fine's records and see that academic records can only be sent to his mother, Corretta Fine, and that Janine Scott introduces herself to you as Carl's father's fiancée?

2. A parent calls during your prep time and asks if he can schedule a conference at the Starbucks in the mall on Saturday morning. The parent says that he can't make the scheduled Friday conference times, and can't be free during any of your prep time, but feels that he must talk in person with you. What is your response?

3. Mrs. Camilla Albright pulls you aside during the first open house at your school and says, "I am the president of the band boosters and the parent serving on the principal's advisory committee this year. I'm also Harry's mom. He's in your fifth-hour class. I wanted you to know that I will do anything to help you out. Just call if you want any background on any of your students or any insider information. I will come by sometime in the next few weeks to observe a class, since I like doing that. Keep me informed about Harry, too, since we want him to go to MIT or Yale." What is your response?

4. Clark Dennison has a 20-minute appointment with you during scheduled conferences. When he arrives, he says in a confrontational tone, "I know that you are the new teacher, so you probably don't understand how grading should be yet. My daughter, Melani, got a B- in your class. She has been an A student until your class. What can you do to help Melani change this grade? I have told her that she will do any extra credit you assign. Do I need to see the principal next?" Your response?

5. After being observed by the curriculum director, she calls you in for a discussion of your class. She says, "Well, the class that I observed looked like something you taught when you were student teaching—all that discussion and open-ended questioning. We have to meet the state standards here, so I need to see direct teaching the next time I observe you for an evaluation." What is your response?

10

SUCCESS STRATEGIES FOR
YOUR FIRST YEAR AND BEYOND

In the past, high school teachers were hired, given the keys to their classrooms, and simply told, "Good luck." Now, with the public accountability to get and keep quality teachers in the classrooms, many schools have implemented orientation, induction, and mentoring programs. Here is what those programs can do for you as a first-year teacher and how you can gain the most from participating in them. If you haven't yet interviewed, be sure and ask the school district about its orientation, induction, and mentoring programs during your interview.

ORIENTATION MEETINGS

Every school has orientation for new and returning teachers, although the length, depth, and value of that orientation vary greatly. New teacher orientation may last from one day to one week; some schools even pay their new hires a bonus for attending. Breakfasts, lunches, and city tours may be included to make the orientation a little more welcoming in nature. During this orientation you will meet the building and district administrators. Always take note of who does what and where their offices are located. You do need to know these people and will need to go to them with questions, concerns, and paperwork. What kinds of information will be covered in orientation?

1. *Paperwork issues:* Employment paperwork, such as income tax forms, health insurance forms, FBI checks, life insurance forms, and emergency contact information. (Districts cannot pay you until *all* the official paperwork is done and your final college transcripts are in the personnel office. This is indeed a motivator to take care of the paperwork.)

2. *Curriculum issues:* The state and district curriculum guides are distributed, with updates on which textbooks and materials are currently being used and how to get them. Announcements of future meetings and where to get help with making the mandated curriculum fit in the amount of time available is very useful information.

3. *Testing:* Districts announce the state and local test dates at the beginning of the year. Mark them on your calendar. Find out if there are practice tests and study guides available and how the other teachers in your field prepare students for high-stakes testing.

4. *Grading:* When will grades be due in the office and how will they be distributed to the students? Will you be required to use a standardized grading system or can you determine your own cutoffs for grades? This is imperative to know before you write your syllabus, units, and letters to parents and students.

5. *Attendance policies:* Schools get their financial support based on the number of students in attendance, so reporting accurate numbers is essential. Also, be sure to know about tardy policies and what you do to report them. The students certainly know the policies and will test you early in the first weeks to see if you know and enforce the policies.

6. *School law:* The legal issues that affect high school teachers include child abuse, drug and alcohol use by students, right to privacy issues, and zero tolerance. Administrators will explain specific issues and policies for the state and district.

7. *Special education/ESOL/gifted education:* Coordinators for each of these programs explain what services are offered and how to get

support for students' special needs. Find out who is in charge and go see them later in the semester for specific questions.

8. *Guidance counselors and social workers:* Because more and more high school students have stress, anxiety, and a myriad of issues, get to know the guidance counselors early and do not hesitate to refer students who need help. If appropriate for your subject area, invite the counselors in to meet with your students for short sessions early in the semester. This is especially important for freshman classes.

9. *Classroom management and discipline referrals:* High schools have policies for in-school suspensions, out-of-school suspensions, and every level of disciplinary action. Make sure you know the school's policies before writing your management plan.

10. *Violence prevention:* Schools have code words for announcements about emergencies, such as "Mr. Jamison, please come to the office," which really means that teachers have to lock their doors and keep every student inside until an all-clear announcement is made. These codes are critically important. The school will probably have a security resource officer who has effective plans in place for violence prevention.

11. *Natural disasters and fire drills:* Remember that student safety takes precedence over all else, and that emergency preparedness is important.

Most of orientation is taken up by listening to speakers give information about policy and procedures. Do not plan to sit in these meetings and do something else, like write lesson plans or prepare a syllabus. As a new teacher, you need this information, and you need to appear attentive and involved because your informal actions at meetings are also a part of your overall evaluation. Be professional. Keep all paperwork where you can find it when you do have a question.

Another part of orientation should be time to work in your classroom, to organize materials and bulletin boards, and to just digest all of the information from the informational meetings. Your orientation should include information about the district's induction and mentoring programs, with time to work with your mentor built into your orientation days.

INDUCTION AND MENTORING

Simply put, induction is the planned staff development for new teachers. The goal of an induction program is to help the new teacher become established, to feel a part of the educational community of the school, and to keep the new teacher from leaving the school or the teaching profession. It is hoped that an induction program will increase the new hire's teaching performance, increase the likelihood of staying in the profession, and promote personal well-being. In other words, an induction program should help a new teacher survive, thrive, and feel happy about teaching, in spite of the many stressors and demands of the job.

Some school districts provide three days of orientation and feel that they have "inducted" their new teachers. However, the best induction programs are ongoing ones, whereby the teachers do not have to give up their own time after school for more meetings. In a model induction program, teachers would be given a half-day of release time once a month for support meetings with other new teachers. With this type of induction, a veteran teacher or a staff developer from the district or a nearby college works with the group throughout the year, sharing teaching tips, management strategies and stress reduction techniques, as well as helping new teachers to fully comprehend all of the policies, procedures, and details involved in working in the district. Some districts provide lunches or dinners for their new teachers and then meet during the meal to provide ideas and support. A district may provide an incentive for attending new teacher workshops by arranging for participants to earn college credit. Find out what is available and take advantage of any opportunities to get help and support. Teaching can be a lonely job, since the high school teacher works in a classroom isolated from other adults most of the day. Reach out to others who are experiencing the same challenges and concerns that you are.

Mentoring is considered a part of induction and is probably more common than ongoing support seminars for newly hired teachers. Mentoring involves the pairing of a new teacher with an experienced teacher. The mentor's role is to help the new teacher become established by answering questions, listening to ideas, providing information about the school policies, and observing some of the classes to provide feedback. A good mentor is a friend, a confidante, a role model, and a person to turn to with your questions. Mentors show new teachers the ins and outs of the school district, while letting them know that their questions and concerns are valid ones shared by other new teachers.

In most districts, the mentor is usually another full-time teacher who teaches down the hall from the new teacher. In some districts, the mentor is a teacher who has been released from his or her own classroom for a year in order to serve as a mentor of many new teachers. Another mentoring model involves recently retired teachers who are hired to mentor a few new teachers in the school as a part-time job. Some districts ask teachers to mentor as a service, without pay, while others pay the teachers for helping new teachers.

How can you get the most from being assigned a mentor? First, find out the guidelines of your district's mentoring program. Know if your mentor is paid to work with you an hour a week or if he or she is volunteering to answer your questions informally. Will you have some time on a regular basis to talk with your mentor and can you develop an agenda of items to discuss? Is your mentor expected to watch you teach a certain number of times and to give you feedback on your teaching? Will your mentor keep your questions confidential or does he or she share information with the principal for your annual evaluation?

Once you know the parameters of your district's program, there are many ways that the mentor can help you. A mentor can

- help you locate books, materials, and supplies.
- share his or her professional library of books and journals.
- discuss ideas for a workable classroom management plan that fits the school's guidelines.
- remind you of school calendar deadlines for grades, book orders, etc.
- discuss the curriculum with you and help you to make long-range plans.
- model some positive stress reduction strategies for you, such as walking during the lunch break or bowling after school on Thursdays.
- share strategies for reaching out to the diverse student population.
- listen to your ideas and provide insight and feedback from his or her own experiences.

However, the mentor is *not* your paraprofessional, secretary, or teacher's aide. It is not the mentor's responsibility to make photocopies for you, or remind you for the third time that nominations for the honor society are due. If your preparation to teach was insufficient in some areas, it is not the mentor's job to teach you an entire course on that subject. For fully certified new teachers, the mentor is a colleague, a resource person, and perhaps an instructional coach. The mentor can help you reflect on your work and celebrate your teaching successes, but does not serve as a magic wizard to solve every problem.

For those who start jobs with provisional teaching certificates, the assigned mentor may have a completely different role. When non-fully certified teachers are hired, they are assigned direct supervisors, who are sometimes called mentors, and their jobs do involve direct teaching of curriculum, methods, and management to the new hire. Whether you are certified or not, your mentor is not the one responsible for your success or failure as a first-year teacher. The mentor is an extra boost, and your first year should be easier because of a mentor.

You can make the most of being assigned a mentor by getting to know that person and the experiences of his or her teaching career. Ask your mentor questions and listen to the answers. Invite him or her into your classroom and ask for feedback on your lesson. Say thank you often. Return books and magazines that have been shared. Attend a professional meeting or carpool to a conference together. Actually, the guidelines for working with your mentor as a colleague will help you to get established with other colleagues as well.

YOUR FIRST EVALUATION

Of course you will be evaluated and you know that being hired for a second year is not automatic. However, you were probably supervised and evaluated more stringently as a student teacher than you may be as a new teacher. Most evaluations consist of the principal or assigned supervisor (assistant principal, curriculum specialist, or department chair) observing two or three of your classes and meeting with you to discuss your overall performance. There are variations, such as a district that has more than three visits and requires an assessment portfolio. Some districts have more than one evaluator and their observations are compared; in addition, a teacher can be asked to identify specific goals for improvement and to complete a self-evaluation.

How do you prepare for an observation/evaluation visit? First, you should receive orientation about the type of observations you will receive. Some districts use a clinical supervision model (see, for example, Glickman, Gordon, & Ross-Gordon, 2004) where the observer meets with you for 20 to 30 minutes to discuss your teaching and to ask you what you feel should be addressed in an observation. Then that supervisor completes an observation, writing out comments of what is seen and perhaps even videotaping the lesson. Afterward, you and the supervisor look at the data collected about your class to identify strengths and weaknesses. This type of supervision has the goal of helping you to reflect on your teaching for improvement of instruction. The biggest advantage of this type of supervision is that visits are announced and that you and the supervisor get to discuss how this lesson relates to previous ones and previous student learning. Since the observer looks for teaching behaviors or student behaviors that you have identified, the observation gives you "another pair of eyes" in the classroom and is actually beneficial, rather than just a perfunctory evaluation of your class with a checklist.

If you will not be supervised with clinical supervision, then the evaluator may just show up at your door with a checklist on a clipboard. You should get a copy of the checklist, which is the evaluation instrument, in advance of the first observation. A typical one will include checking to see if your room is well organized and neat, if bulletin boards are current, if rules are posted, and if there are places in the room for students to find out what work they missed when out. Once the evaluator examines your use of the room, then he or she will watch you teach and look for the following:

- Introduction to the lesson
- Engagement of students (are they on-task?)
- The quality of how you present new material
- Your use of questions and activities to engage students
- Your use of time (keeping students busy from bell to bell)
- Student behavior—discipline problems will be noted
- Assessment of student learning throughout the lesson

- Conclusion of the lesson
- Your interest and enthusiasm
- Your short- and long-term planning

If your district uses one model of teaching, then that model will probably be used for the evaluation. For example, throughout the 1980s teachers learned about Madeline Hunter's seven-step lesson plan. They were then evaluated with a checklist that contained her seven steps. If they missed a step, the evaluation was lower (Hunter, 1994). A high school where I supervise student teachers insists that the state-mandated curriculum goal be listed on the board every day, in order that the students know what they are learning and that the teacher meets the state goal. In addition, that school requires that an "essential question" be written on the board for every lesson. The question focuses students' learning and is a reminder that they must learn an answer to that question by the end of the class. Failure to have those two items written on the board would certainly lower an evaluation. Many districts also have schoolwide discipline policies, and each teacher must post a set of rules with consequences and punishments on a poster in the room. Teachers are evaluated on whether their posters are in place, and if they contain appropriate rules. The bottom line is that you need to know the guidelines for evaluations *before* the semester begins and what the observer will be expecting when he or she visits your room. If your orientation does not include guidelines for evaluations, then ask your mentor or principal for them.

The best way to get a good first evaluation is to be doing your job well. When a supervisor visits, have a lesson plan that he or she can read while watching you teach. Share a copy of the book to look at, copies of handouts, and make sure that your students see visuals of what you are teaching. If you look disorganized or uninterested when the supervisor is there, what must your class be like when you are not being observed?

PORTFOLIOS AND OTHER DOCUMENTATION

If a portfolio is required during your first year of teaching, find out early in the year what is required. Good things to keep for a portfolio include:

- a sample letter sent to parents about your management plan
- a sample letter sent to parents about the curriculum
- lesson plans that worked well
- original outlines, worksheets, quizzes, and tests that you designed
- units that you created
- samples of student work, with the names removed
- photos of bulletin boards
- photos of students working and presenting their work
- positive notes from students and their parents
- a copy of observations from mentors and evaluators
- proof of attendance at some extracurricular events

As scary as an evaluation of any kind may be, remember that your administrators want you to succeed. Replacing any new teacher can be very time consuming for the administrator, and schools with high employee turnover look bad. So, if you are discouraged after your first evaluations, ask your boss for specific feedback on ways to improve. Part of your boss's job is to help you succeed.

STOCKING YOUR FIRST CLASSROOM WITH SUPPLIES

Teachers need a lot of "stuff" for teaching, and supplies are *not* all available from your school. However, do not buy anything until you know whether or not your school already has it. Sometimes that means you will need to scrounge around for supplies and find the right person to ask for things you need. What do you need? In addition to textbooks, a whiteboard, markers, an overhead projector, paper, and a computer, you may need lots of little things to make your room a better workplace for you and the students. Here are some things that veteran teachers keep on hand:

- extension cord
- electric fan
- magazines and paperback books to keep students busy who finish early (sorted for suitability)
- clean T-shirts for you or a student (saves a trip home for anyone who spills or students who might get suspended for a graphic T-shirt worn to school)

- old sweaters/sweatshirts to lend to students if room is too cold
- CD player, with earphones, can be used to reward a student who finishes early
- thank-you cards and postcards to send parents, students, and volunteers
- a few dollars to "loan" for student lunch and emergencies
- tissues
- hand lotion
- paper, pens, markers, crayons, scissors
- art supplies

A first-year teacher's salary will only stretch so far, so be creative. Try flea markets and garage sales for some of these items. Your parents' attic or basement may have some great finds. My mother gave me some board games and a bingo game that I adapted for Spanish and used for over a decade in teaching. Recently retired teachers sometimes want to share their accumulations of teacher stuff with new teachers, too. Many teachers send out letters to parents asking for donations at the beginning of the year. Be careful with this approach, as some parents resent being asked to supply their school in addition to paying their property/school taxes and student fees. Never send such a letter without the explicit consent of your school administration.

With the basic supplies on hand for your room, it's time to look at a checklist of things to get yourself organized. Find out how early you can work in your new classroom and take this checklist with you to set up your classroom. (For more ideas, see, for example, Rominger, Laughrea, & Elkin, 2001; see worksheet 10.1).

PERSONAL LIFE

What about your personal life? How do you prepare personally to not only survive in the teaching profession but to balance work and home so that you feel happy and well? While the general public perceives teaching as an "easy" 8-to-3 job, real teachers know differently. Yes, the first few years of teaching do require more time than later years in terms of preparation, but every year requires a lot of time, and the job simply

_____ 1. Count the desks and compare to your rolls to see if you have enough desks.

_____ 2. Arrange the desks so that you can walk around to each.

_____ 3. Find a good place for your desk, as well as an entrance table, so students can pick up info as they walk in to the room.

_____ 4. Find the textbooks and bring enough to your room for students.

_____ 5. Get a copy of every emergency policy and post them (fire, tornado, evacuation, etc.)

_____ 6. Get a good calendar for yourself and pencil in all of the meetings, due dates for grades, and the vacations.

_____ 7. Make a bulletin board that posts the important dates for students, especially seniors.

_____ 8. Post your management plan.

_____ 9. Get some file folders and plan drawers for keeping student work, lesson ideas, and extra teaching activities.

_____ 10. Get some kind of bins or "in and out" boxes for collecting student work and giving students access to makeup work. A box with file folders for each student works well.

_____ 11. Make your seating charts.

_____ 12. Keep one spot for your office mail and memos from the office.

_____ 13. Keep one file of important handouts from the school office.

Worksheet 10.1. Organizational Checklist for Setting Up Your Classroom

cannot be done well without putting in some extra time. What is a committed professional to do?

First of all, be realistic. There are only 24 hours in a day and only seven days in a week. If you have a spouse and/or children, enlist their support for help during the school year. Keep a calendar for the whole family and communicate time needs, duties, and responsibilities. I know teachers whose mothers come and clean their houses (for pay) and whose children actually cook and do laundry. While teaching is the "family friendly" profession, there are still time constraints. You have to get your personal life organized in order to feel comfortable about your teaching life. Everyone in education has heard that you shouldn't get married your first year of teaching or have a baby that first year. While it is certainly your right to do those things, you may want to balance your life by getting established, then adding new roles to your life. The decisions are yours. Teaching part-time or subbing has been an answer for some new teachers who are newlyweds, new parents, and new teachers simultaneously. In fact, teaching part-time has helped some single new teachers "get their feet on the ground" too.

You know your own internal clock. Some teachers work best in the mornings and come in early to get work done. Others stay late and then don't take work home. A third group takes work home so that they can leave at a reasonable hour and do household chores while grading papers or planning. I always take Saturdays off, but work on Sunday afternoons until the work is done. A friend of mine likes to work on Saturday mornings until she is prepared for the next week, and then celebrates with movie and dinner out on Saturday night and a free Sunday. Again, each person must find his or her own answer, but there has to be an answer and a plan. Teaching is not an 8-to-3 job just because our classes are taught at those times. Be prepared for some long days and some necessary attendance at extracurricular events.

STRESS MANAGEMENT

Are today's teachers stressed? You don't have to do formal research to answer that question with a "yes." Teaching can be a very stressful profession, but it is also a very rewarding one, and one in which the individual classroom teacher can establish an environment to lower stress for both herself and the students. What are the keys to stress management? Most experts agree that basic good health components can help reduce stress.

- Eat a balanced diet, limiting caffeine.
- Drink lots of water.
- Strive for several hours of sleep a night—most of us need eight hours.
- Exercise three times a week.
- Take a few minutes every day for yourself, even if those few minutes are just a longer shower, bath, or a second cup of tea.
- Have a support network of family and friends.

These basics are so simple, but what about more advanced stress management? When you feel stressed, you have to identify the areas of your work and personal life that are the causes of your stress and then you have to find a way to make a change in the areas causing stress. Once the problem and solution are identified, then you must make the change. For example, one teacher reported that she was terribly stressed every November, not by school, but by having to host a family Thanksgiving meal for over 25 people. The extra cooking and cleaning were stressful, as well as the fact that she felt other family members did not do their fair share. The teacher paid $200 to go to a stress management workshop and was told, "You have identified the cause. Now find a solution. How about telling the family you simply cannot host the dinner? If you feel you could host the dinner if everyone else brought food and you supplied the location, then do that. Or even suggest that everyone meet in restaurant or community room. There are options. You can say no or make changes." The teacher wasn't sure she could make any of those changes, but the stress wouldn't be solved without a change. Use the following questionnaire to identify stressors and possible solutions (see worksheet 10.2).

Another good activity for stress management is to identify the things that you can control and the things that you can't. Start by listing the things you control about your own classroom, then progress to personal issues. If you can control the issue, seize power and do so! If not,

A. Where is the problem? On a scale of 0 to 10, where 0 indicates no stress and 10 indicates high stress, rate the following teacher concerns:

1. Communicating and dealing with parents. _____
2. Communicating and dealing with colleagues. _____
3. Communicating and dealing with administrators. _____
4. Presenting and teaching the subject matter. _____
5. Classroom management and discipline. _____
6. Working with inclusion students without support. _____
7. Too many students in my class. _____
8. Physical classroom—size, heat, cleanliness. _____
9. Motivating students to work. _____
10. Not having enough supplies/books. _____
11. Keeping up with paper grading/grading students' work. _____
12. Dealing with students' social and emotional problems. _____
13. Dealing with students' substance abuse problems. _____
14. Dealing with criticism from the public about teaching. _____
15. Standardized tests and accountability programs at school. _____
16. My continued employment. _____

And now rate the following personal concerns with regard to your stress:

1. Not enough time with my family/spouse/children. _____
2. Not enough time to socialize with friends/date. _____
3. Not enough time to relax and do nothing. _____
4. Dealing with parents or in-laws. _____
5. Money/financial concerns. _____
6. My own health issues. _____
7. Health issues of immediate family members. _____

Worksheet 10.2. The ABCs of Stress Management Survey

8. Concerns about my children's quality of life. _____

9. Household cooking, cleaning, chores, laundry. _____

10. Live where the climate/weather is difficult. _____

List any more stressors not mentioned above and rate.

B. List all of the concerns that you rated a 6 or higher. Now, list a solution to that problem. For example, if dealing with students' behavior is a stressor, can you get some additional training in management and discipline, or start a discussion group with other teachers who have the same concerns?

C. You have to do the action outlined in part B to address the stressor. Good luck!

Worksheet 10.2. *(continued)*

you may have to quit berating yourself for feeling stressed over that issue.

Answer the following questions on a card and post it on your refrigerator or keep it handy on your desk at school for more stress relief reminders:

1. Something nice that I do for myself every day is . . .
   every week is . . .
   every semester is . . .
2. I want to make an effort to spend more time every day doing . . .
3. When things get really difficult at school, I can . . .
4. The part of teaching that I enjoy the most is . . . and I will strive to concentrate on that.

It is important to remember that what resolves the stress of one person may cause stress for another. One teacher kept a bag of small chocolate kisses in her desk and rewarded herself with one at the end of each day. While this worked well for her, it wouldn't work for those of us who might eat the whole bag at the end of a hectic day! Another teacher gardened to reduce her stress. Gardening might *cause* stress if I had to do it! In other words, stress reduction techniques are very personalized.

Perhaps one of the best ways to reduce stress is to build a network of professional teachers. You will not be the only teacher in America who is struggling with teaching grammar or who has concerns over getting students motivated to read the classics. Reach out and ask others what they are doing. Attend workshops given by the professional associations in your area. Sometimes getting more involved, rather than retreating into isolation, will help resolve stress. (See the chapter on curriculum for the national organizations of each subject area and the chapter on technology for other organizations for teachers.)

SUCCESS

A colleague of mine always asks the same question to candidates in job interviews, "Five years from now, how will you know if you have been successful?" As teachers, we should perhaps ask ourselves this more often. Success may mean that we are still gainfully employed and helping our students. Success may mean that more of our students are graduating than before we joined the faculty. Success may mean that we have finished a master's degree or produced a portfolio for consideration for National Board Certification. The following poem illustrates one idea of success and knowing why we teach. The author is unknown and the poem was found on a small poster in a gift shop.

> I teach because I see the hope
> An education brings.
> Because the treasures found in books
> Give children stronger wings.
> I can't replace the parents
> Of those I see each day
> But I can teach and gently coax
> Young hearts who come my way.

The secret to teaching may be in finding that the little successes are truly big successes. If this is your first year or your thirty-first year, be idealistic and give students hope through education.

REFERENCES

Anderson, L. W. (2003). *Classroom assessment: Enhancing the quality of teacher decision making*. Mahwah, NJ: Lawrence Erlbaum.

Arends, R. I. (1994). *Learning to teach* (3rd ed.). New York: McGraw-Hill.

Bennett, C. I. (2003). *Comprehensive multicultural education: Theory and practice* (5th ed.). Boston: Allyn & Bacon.

Bonwell, C. C. & Eison, J. A. (1991). *Active learning: Creating excitement in the classroom*. ASHE-ERIC Higher Education Report No. 1. Washington, DC: George Washington University/ERIC Clearinghouse.

Callahan, J. F., Clark, L. H., & Kellough, R. D. (1998). Teaching in the middle and secondary schools (6th ed.). Upper Saddle River, NJ: Merrill.

Callahan, J. F., Clark, L. H., & Kellough, R. D. (2002). *Teaching in the middle and secondary schools* (7th ed.). Upper Saddle River, NJ: Merrill Prentice Hall.

Campbell, B. (1994). *The multiple intelligences handbook: Lesson plans and more*. Stanwood, WA: Campbell and Associates.

Canter, L. & Canter, M. (2001). *Assertive discipline: Positive behavior management for today's classroom*, (3rd ed). Los Angeles: Canter & Associates.

Canter, L. & Garrison, R. (1994). *Scared or prepared: Preventing conflict and violence in your classroom*. Los Angeles: Canter & Associates.

Clement, M. C. (2002). What cooperating teachers are teaching student teachers about classroom management. *The Teacher Educator, 38*(1), 47–62.

Cruikshank, D. R., Bainer, D., & Metcalf, K. (1995). *The act of teaching.* New York: McGraw-Hill.

Curwin, R. L. & Mendler, A. N. (1988). *Discipline with dignity.* Alexandria, VA: Association for Supervision and Curriculum Development.

Davidman, L. & Davidman, P. T. (2001). *Teaching with a multicultural perspective: A practical guide* (3rd ed.). New York: Longman.

Dewey, J. (1998). *Experience and education: The 60th anniversary edition.* West Lafayette, IN: Kappa Delta Pi.

Emmer, E. T., Evertson, C. M., & Worsham, M. E. (1999). *Classroom management for the secondary teacher* (5th ed.). Boston: Allyn & Bacon.

Erwin, J. C. (2003). Giving students what they need. *Educational Leadership, 61*(1), 19–23.

Evertson, C. M., Emmer, E. T., Clements, B. S., & Worsham, M. E. (1997). *Classroom management for elementary teachers.* Boston: Allyn & Bacon.

Gabler, I. C. & Schroeder, M. (2003). *Constructivist methods for the secondary classroom: Engaged minds.* Boston: Allyn & Bacon.

Glickman, C. D., Gordon, S. P., & Ross-Gordon, J. M. (2004). *Supervision and instructional leadership: A developmental approach* (6th ed.). Boston: Allyn & Bacon.

Hunter, M. (1994). *Enhancing teaching.* New York: Macmillan College.

Johnson, N. L. (1990). *Questioning makes the difference.* Beavercreek, OH: Creative Learning Consultants.

Joyce, B. & Weil, M. (1986). *Models of teaching* (3rd ed.). Englewood Cliffs, NJ: Prentice-Hall.

Kellough, R. D. & Kellough, N. G. (1999). *Secondary school teaching: A guide to methods and resources: Planning for competence.* Upper Saddle River, NJ: Merrill.

Kellough, R. D. & Kellough, N. G. (2003). *Secondary school teaching: A guide to methods and resources: Planning for competence* (2nd ed.). Upper Saddle River, NJ: Merrill.

Kozminsky, E. & Kozminsky, L. (2003). Improving motivation through dialogue. *Educational Leadership, 61*(1), 50–54.

Marzano, R. J., Marzano, J. S., & Pickering, D. J. (2003). *Classroom management that works: Research-based strategies for every teacher.* Alexandria, VA: Association for Supervision and Curriculum Development.

Nieto, S. (2000). *Affirming diversity: The sociopolitical context of multicultural education* (3rd ed.). New York: Longman.

Orlich, D. C., Kauchak, D. P., Harder, R. J., Pendergrass, R. A., Callahan, R. C., Keogh, A. J., & Gibson, H. (1990). *Teaching strategies: A guide to better instruction* (3rd ed.). Lexington, MA: D. C. Heath.

Palmer, P. J. (1998). *The courage to teach.* San Francisco: Jossey-Bass.

Rominger, L., Laughrea, S. P., & Elkin, N. (2001). *Your first year as a high school teacher.* Roseville, CA: Prima.

Starnes, B. A. & Carone, A. (2002). *From thinking to doing: The Foxfire core practices.* Mountain City, GA: Foxfire Fund.

Walker, D. E. (1998). *Strategies for teaching differently on the block or not.* Thousand Oaks, CA: Corwin Press.

Wardle, F. & Cruz-Janzen, M. I. (2004). *Meeting the needs of multiethnic and multiracial children in schools.* Boston: Pearson/Allyn & Bacon.

Wigginton, E. (1985). *Sometimes a shining moment.* New York: Doubleday.

Winebrenner, S. (1992). *Teaching gifted kids in the regular classroom.* Minneapolis: Free Spirit.

Wong, H. K. & Wong, R. T. (1998). *How to be an effective teacher: The first days of school.* Mountain View, CA: Harry K. Wong.

Wormeli, R. (2001). *Meet me in the middle: Becoming an accomplished middle-level teacher.* Portland, ME: Stenhouse.

INDEX

ABOUT THE AUTHOR

Mary C. Clement was a high school foreign language teacher for eight years before earning a doctorate in curriculum and instruction from the University of Illinois at Urbana-Champaign in 1991. She directed the Beginning Teacher Program at Eastern Illinois University for six years and is now an associate professor of teacher education at Berry College in northwest Georgia.

Clement's teaching includes secondary curriculum and methods, foreign language methods, and classroom management. She teaches graduate courses in curriculum theory and supervision and mentoring. Her articles have appeared in the *Kappan*, *Principal Leadership*, the *Clearinghouse*, and Kappa Delta Pi's *Educational Record* and *Forum*. She is the author of *Building the Best Faculty* and *So You Want to Be a Teacher?* also from ScarecrowEducation.